Sex Work

Sexuality Studies Series

This series focuses on original, provocative, scholarly research examining from a range of perspectives the complexity of human sexual practice, identity, community, and desire. Books in the series explore how sexuality interacts with other aspects of society, such as law, education, feminism, racial diversity, the family, policing, sport, government, religion, mass media, medicine, and employment. The series provides a broad public venue for nurturing debate, cultivating talent, and expanding knowledge of human sexual expression, past and present.

Other volumes in the series are:

Sex Work

Rethinking the Job,
Respecting the Workers

COLETTE PARENT, CHRIS BRUCKERT,
PATRICE CORRIVEAU, MARIA NENGEH MENSAH,
and LOUISE TOUPIN

Translated by Käthe Roth

UBCPress · Vancouver · Toronto

Originally published as *Mais oui c'est un travail! Penser le travail du sexe au-delà de la victimisation* © Les Presses de l'Université du Québec 2010

Library and Archives Canada Cataloguing in Publication

Mais oui c'est un travail! English
    Sex work : rethinking the job, respecting the workers / Colette Parent, Chris Bruckert, Patrice Corriveau, Maria Nengeh Mensah, and Louise Toupin ; translated by Käthe Roth.

(Sexuality studies series)
Translation of: Mais oui c'est un travail!
Includes bibliographical references and index.
Issued in print and electronic formats.
ISBN 978-0-7748-2611-2 (bound). – ISBN 978-0-7748-2612-9 (pbk.). – ISBN 978-0-7748-2613-6 (pdf). – ISBN 978-0-7748-2614-3 (epub).

    1. Prostitution. 2. Victims of crimes. 3. Human trafficking. 4. Prostitutes – Civil rights. I. Parent, Colette, 1947-, author II. Title. III. Series: Sexuality studies series.

HQ118.M3413 2013   306.74   C2013-903399-8
                                                       C2013-903400-5

Canada

UBC Press gratefully acknowledges the financial support for our publishing program of the Government of Canada (through the Canada Book Fund), the Canada Council for the Arts, and the British Columbia Arts Council.

This book has been published with the help of a grant from the Canadian Federation for the Humanities and Social Sciences, through the Awards to Scholarly Publications Program, using funds provided by the Social Sciences and Humanities Research Council of Canada. We acknowledge the financial support of the Government of Canada, through the National Translation Program for Book Publishing, for our translation activities.

UBC Press
The University of British Columbia
2029 West Mall
Vancouver, BC V6T 1Z2
www.ubcpress.ca

Canada Council   Conseil des arts
for the Arts   du Canada

Recognizing that the violence must end, recognizing that even in our history of horrors we have struck our blows and that, wanted or not, these terrible stories are not the majority. There are many good stories, many. And many of simple daily lives – bus job bed. And yes, recognizing that we know what we need. Then, perhaps sitting down together to advance, my sisters. To dig up the murderers. Because all women, transsexuals, and transvestites who are harassed or assaulted are treated as whores, it seems to me, offer the prospect of fighting to change what being a whore symbolizes. Because we exist. Millions of women breadwinners. The right to live, to be protected, to be respected.

— ROXANNE NADEAU, "PAROLE DE PUTE" (our translation)

Contents

Abbreviations

CATW	Coalition Against Trafficking in Women (formerly International Feminist Network Against Sexual Slavery and Trafficking in Women)
CEDREF	Centre d'enseignement, de documentation et de recherches pour les études féministes
CORP	Canadian Organization for the Rights of Prostitutes
COYOTE	Call Off Your Old Tired Ethics
CRI-VIFF	Centre de recherche interdisciplinaire sur la violence familiale et la violence faite aux femmes
DMSC	Durbar Mahila Samanwaya Committee
FPT Working Group	Federal/Provincial/Territorial Working Group on Prostitution
GAATW	Global Alliance Against Traffic in Women
IOM	International Organization for Migration
NGO	Non-governmental organization

NOW	National Organization for Women
OIM	Organisation internationale pour les migrations
PAFR	Programme des aides familiaux résidants
PROS	Providers and Resources Offering Services to Sex Workers
RCMP	Royal Canadian Mounted Police
TAMPEP	European Network for HIV/STI Prevention and Health Promotion among Migrant Sex Workers
UN	United Nations
UNAIDS	Joint United Nations Programme on HIV/AIDS
USAID	United States Agency for International Development
US GAO	US Government Accountability Office

Sex Work

Introduction

COLETTE PARENT, CHRIS BRUCKERT, PATRICE CORRIVEAU,
MARIA NENGEH MENSAH, and LOUISE TOUPIN

Canadian media and justice spokespeople have called Port Coquitlam farmer Robert Pickton the worst serial killer in the country's history: in 2007, he was found guilty of murdering six women and feeding their cadavers to his pigs, and charged with twenty other murders. Pickton admitted to having killed forty-nine women to an undercover agent sharing his prison cell. Most of his victims were "prostitutes" who performed sex work in the east-end neighbourhood of Vancouver, British Columbia.

Today, Pickton is behind bars, sentenced to life in prison with no possibility of parole for twenty-five years. Nevertheless, our collective memory remains shaken by this sordid affair, which highlighted not only the physical violence that an individual may perpetrate on marginalized people, but also the violence of prejudices against female sex workers. These prejudices still threaten to surface and provide fodder for the argument against sex work. This is so true that we actually hesitated to mention the Pickton affair in this introduction, for fear of reviving repressive attitudes or perpetuating a generalized dominant discourse that reduces female sex workers to victims, without pointing out their strengths and legitimacy or recognizing their activism.

In fact, since the 1990s, sex work has figured in the Canadian political and media arenas mainly through two *victimizing* portrayals of this form of work: first, a focus on trafficking in women for the purposes of "prostitution"; second, a highlighting of the physical vulnerability of female sex workers, brought to light by the Pickton affair. The people most responsible for promulgating this attitude promote a vision that is predominant around the world, that of prohibitionists and the "morals police," including many feminists who object to "the prostitution of women by men."

With regard to trafficking in women for the purposes of "prostitution," Canada quickly fell in line with the international community by adopting laws to combat what has been defined as a problem of exploitation of individuals rather than the unauthorized migration of workers. Very few female sex workers in Canada are known to have been victims of human trafficking. In a number of countries, however, migrant women looking for work are regularly confronted with obstacles to their mobility: they are not allowed to travel alone, without the approval of their fathers or husbands, or they are unable to obtain a passport or travel visa. These women face prejudices, restrictive – even racist – immigration policies, or the outright closing of borders.

The other issue that has surfaced in Canada since the 1990s is the portrayal of sex work through the lens of the vulnerability of female sex workers. Behind the tragedy represented by serial killers, there is the tragedy of a society that harbours the idea that female sex workers "ask for it" when men, psychopaths or not, rape or kill them because they are perceived to have exposed themselves to danger. In New Zealand, where sex work has been decriminalized, working conditions have clearly become safer. So why does Canada let these tragedies take place among the most vulnerable female sex workers, those who labour in precarious working conditions such as the street?

The person who may have been Pickton's first victim disappeared in the early 1990s; it took until 2002 for the net to tighten around him. Only in 2005 did the Parliament of Canada, at the request of MP Libby Davis, form the Subcommittee on Solicitation Laws of the Standing Committee on Justice, Human Rights, Public Security, and Emergency Preparedness. Dissolved when a federal election was called, the subcommittee was re-formed in 2006, but its deliberations resulted in no change to the law that might have better protected the physical integrity of female sex workers.

Today, it seems that the rights of female sex workers to life and the possibility of earning a living are no longer of interest to public decision makers in Canada, although three courageous female sex workers recently mounted a legal challenge in Ontario Superior Court in an attempt to invalidate the provisions of the *Criminal Code* related to "prostitution."[1] In the meantime, these provisions are still in force; governmental authorities support initiatives aimed at stamping out "prostitution" and renew statutes that, once again, penalize female sex workers.

To keep these workers' voices and the defence of their rights and interests from being obscured again, we decided to produce this book on sex work. Between the five of us, we have accumulated many years of activism, and our respective writings have contributed to the development of scholarship on sex work on a number of levels.

On the theoretical level, in a chapter in *Traité des problèmes sociaux* published in 1994, Colette Parent emphasized the need to think of the question of "prostitution" from within the world of female sex workers. This article broke new ground by addressing the subject in the French Canadian scholarly field in the 1990s. Parent asserted the need for the fields of criminology, feminist studies, and sociology to revise analyses and come up with solutions in collaboration with the principals concerned, and her work inspired a number of studies. On the ethnographic level, Chris Bruckert's research has unveiled the complexity of women's work in the world of professional strippers. Bruckert had been a sex worker, and she shed light, from a feminist standpoint, on the fact that the female sex worker is in fact the author and not the "object" of her experience.[2] On the level of Canadian governmental interventions, Patrice Corriveau has played a key role as a senior analyst of criminal policies in the Department of Justice Canada. In this role, among others, he has developed a keen comprehension of the field of criminal policies within governmental agencies and acquired solid knowledge of the specific issues related to the question of sex work in each Canadian province.[3] Maria Nengeh Mensah has collaborated closely with groups of sex workers in Canada and elsewhere since 1998.[4] In particular, she has participated in setting up numerous community initiatives the goal of which is to dismantle some of the dynamics of social exclusion that sex workers face, including the training of social workers regarding the issue. Finally, on the international level, Louise Toupin has discussed conventions on trafficking in women and the resulting forms of feminist intervention. Her analyses are aligned with the critical reversals in this field of activity, which reformulate the problems of "prostitution" and human trafficking in terms of the right to mobility and the right to work from the point of view of those experiencing them.[5]

It is thus from these respective fields of expertise that we share with readers our vision of sex work. To date, no book considering "prostitution" as a form of work has been published in a French Canadian context. This is the point of view that we put forward in this book.

Before we go on, we want to clarify our use of certain concepts. First, readers will already have noticed that we use the word "prostitution" in quotation marks. It is a term that we feel is stigmatizing, and we have decided to put it in quotation marks to distance ourselves from that stigma. We prefer the terms "sex work," "work in the sex industry," and "work in erotic establishments," which do not bear this moral weight.

Second, the notions of abolitionism and neo-abolitionism have very particular significance in the field of "prostitution." Commonly, when the concept of abolitionism is evoked, we think of abolition of slavery or of the death penalty. During the second half of the nineteenth century in the West, however, this term was used in the debate over criminal policies with regard to "prostitution." This debate was kept in the public eye due to government concerns, and abolition was one of the issues on the moral reform platform that emerged late in that century. In this context, the definition of the word changed.

As a point of departure, in both the United States and England,[6] feminists fought to abolish the regulation of "prostitution" and eventually to abolish the sex trade by raising the moral values of all citizens. But by the end of the nineteenth century, when the question of regulation was no longer on the political agenda, abolitionists were demanding the elimination of "prostitution" as such. Reformers, including feminists, advocated the use of laws that would affect all "prostitution" activities by targeting every facet of the trade and all the actors involved, including female "prostitutes." This moral reform movement was active in a number of Western countries, including Canada, until between 1917 and 1920.

The neo-abolitionist movement emerged during the first two decades of the twentieth century in the wake of the globalization of markets and increased migration of workers, including female sex workers, to other countries in search of a living. These migrants, the vast majority without papers, were vulnerable to different forms of exploitation and human trafficking. The issue raised interest and indignation in numerous countries, and the League of Nations was mobilized to fight the problem. It was in this context that the neo-abolitionists defined "prostitution" as a form of violence and demanded that it be stamped out. Casting female sex workers as victims, the neo-abolitionists wanted to remove them from the criminal system and proposed criminalization of other facets of "prostitution" activities, targeting in particular the customers and pimps.

We want to convey the vision of "prostitution" as work, respect the voices of female sex workers, and oppose the neo-abolitionist message that presents sex workers as victims of pimps or of their own false consciousness. Our book addresses the main elements of the debate in five chapters.

In the first chapter, Colette Parent and Chris Bruckert present the current debate on sex work. After giving a brief overview of the historical background of the debate, they summarize the main ideas behind the two dominant positions and hold them up to the evidence of empirical research and the voices of female sex workers. In the second chapter, Patrice Corriveau presents the various legal models for controlling "prostitution" and their limitations. He advocates decriminalization of sex work and deconstructs the arguments advanced by proponents of a repressive approach. The third chapter addresses the organization of labour in certain sectors of the sex industry (street work, massage parlours, erotic establishments). Chris Bruckert and Colette Parent describe the skills needed to practise the trade and the challenges that female sex workers face on a daily basis, thus opening the door to an analysis of the social stigmatization of and impact of laws on this type of work. The fourth chapter, by Maria Nengeh Mensah, gives an overall view of

the activism and initiatives of female sex workers in a number of countries, taking as a point of departure Forum XXX on sex work, held in
Montreal in 2005. Mensah highlights the main demands of different
groups, the recognition and legitimacy of associations advocating for
better working conditions, and the potential for alliances between female
sex workers and other groups. She demonstrates once again the importance of working on this issue with those who are most concerned. In
the final chapter, Louise Toupin takes inspiration from a series of empirical studies conducted with migrant women since the 1990s and
answers a number of common questions about the phenomenon of
"trafficking" or "trade" in women. Often confused in the media with
illegal migration by women for the purpose of sex work, this dominant
discourse has harmful consequences for all migrant women, in addition
to providing fodder for anti-migration policies. Toupin deconstructs
certain received ideas on this issue and highlights some practices promoted by organizations of female sex workers working directly with the
migrant women affected.

In the pages that follow, we hope to deconstruct certain myths and
prejudices and to argue convincingly that it is not only possible but
necessary to defend the legitimacy of sex work while fighting violence
against sex workers.

Notes

1 In 2009, Terry-Jean Bedford and female sex workers Valerie Scott, fifty-one years
old, and Amy Lebovitch, thirty years old, asked the Ontario Superior Court to void
the provisions of the *Criminal Code* related to prostitution because they infringe
on the Canadian Charter of Rights and Freedoms. These women felt that they were
forced to put their lives in danger because the law forbade the opening of brothels,
which would enable female sex workers to work under much safer conditions.
2 See Bruckert (2002) and Bruckert and Parent (2007).
3 See Corriveau (2008).
4 See Mensah (2006)
5 See Toupin (2002).
6 For the United States, see Rosen (1982); for England, see Dubois and Gordon (1983)
and Walkowitz (1991).

References

Bruckert, Chris. 2002. *Taking It Off, Putting It On: Women in the Strip Trade.* Toronto: Women's Press.

Bruckert, Chris, and Colette Parent. 2007. La danse érotique comme métier à l'ère de la vente de soi. *Cahiers de recherche sociologique* 43: 97-109.

Bruckert, Chris, Colette Parent, and Daniel Pouliot. 2005. *Comment répondre aux besoins des travailleuses du sexe de rue dans la région de l'Outaouais.* Ottawa: Status of Women.

Corriveau, Patrice. 2008. L'évolution de la gestion juridique des individus aux moeurs homoérotiques au Québec: l'influence des discours dominants. *Bulletin d'histoire politique* 16 (3): 33-42.

Dubois, Ellen Carol, and Linda Gordon. 1983. Seeking Ecstasy on the Battlefield: Danger and Pleasure in Nineteenth-Century Feminist Sexual Thought. *Feminist Studies* 9 (1): 7-25.

McKeganey, Neil P., and Marina Barnard. 1996. *Sex Work on the Streets: Prostitutes and Their Clients.* London: Open University Press Buckingham.

Mensah, Maria Nengeh. 2006. Débats féministes sur la prostitution au Québec, point de vue des travailleuses du sexe. *Revue canadienne de sociologie et d'anthropologie* 43 (3): 346-61.

Parent, Colette. 1994. La "prostitution" ou le commerce des services sexuels. In *Traité des problèmes sociaux*, ed. Simon Langlois, Yves Martin, and Fernand Dumont, 393-407. Quebec City: Institut québécois de recherche sur la culture.

Rosen, Ruth. 1982. *The Lost Sisterhood: Prostitution in America, 1900-1918.* Baltimore and London: Johns Hopkins University Press.

Toupin, Louise. 2002. La scission politique du féminisme international sur la question du "traffic des femmes": vers la "migration" d'un certain féminisme radical? *Recherches féministes* 15 (3/4): 9-40.

Walkowitz, Judith R. 1991. Sexualités dangereuses. In *Histoires des femmes en Occident, Le xixe siècle*, ed. George Duby, Michelle Perrot, and Geneviève Fraisse, 389-418. Paris: Plon.

The Current Debate on Sex Work   1

COLETTE PARENT AND CHRIS BRUCKERT

All too often, in current discussions on sex work, the arguments appear to be driven by emotion. To uncover the foundations of the different positions and distinguish them from the ideological and moral dimensions in which they are cloaked, we must take a step back from the fiery polemics. With this focus in mind, we present certain reflections on the history of contemporary conceptions of "prostitution" in the West, and we then discuss the foundational arguments of the two antagonistic positions that currently dominate the debate.

The Heritage of the Nineteenth Century and the Feminist Movement of the 1960s

In the second half of the nineteenth century, in both England and its Canadian colony, the "problem" of sex work was in the political foreground. Some citizens – politicians, doctors, judges, and journalists – were advocating that this "necessary evil"[1] be controlled through the adoption of regulations that would protect "health, decency, and public order." Others, the first "prostitution" abolitionists, defined sex work as a scourge to be eradicated and proposed that a myriad of statutes be enacted to fight all of the activities involved. Finally, members of religious and parish associations directed their attention to the "prostitutes" themselves, defined as victims, and created shelters designed to help them change their path. Without women working in the trade, these people believed, "prostitution" would peter out. Following numerous debates, harsher laws were implemented, exacerbating the isolation and vulnerability of female sex workers.[2] This wave of repression, which extended to the end of the nineteenth century, left its mark on current Canadian criminal policy.[3]

During this period, middle-class feminists became interested in "prostitution."[4] Their contribution to the debate, however, reflected the ambiguity of their position. First, they defined "prostitution" as an activity resorted to on a temporary basis by working-class women who had to provide the essentials for themselves and their families. It was thus considered a transitory response to the imperative of economic survival. Then, these feminists made a distinction between "prostitution"-related activities and other types of work. They observed that female sex workers were subjected to the double standard of morality by gender[5] at the same time that they were condemned for their choice of livelihood, even if it was a question of survival. In the feminists' view, the solution to the problem was twofold: first, the laws responsible for marginalization of these women had to be abolished; second, over the longer term, men had to become as virtuous as women and transform themselves into faithful husbands. Up to this point, therefore, middle-class feminists supported female sex workers.

But during the 1870s, this view was overshadowed by the emergence of a moral reform movement, and the feminist position changed. Replacing the image of women offering sexual services as a response to their social and economic predicament was that of young, innocent victims, seduced and betrayed, overwhelmed with hunger, or even subjected to physical violence. Feminists now considered sex work to be a form of slavery. The situation was deemed intolerable, and reformers proposed a merciless fight against those responsible: depraved noblemen and profiteers, many of them unscrupulous foreigners. The response to the victimization of women by these immoral men was to be found in the adoption of more numerous and more severe laws. However, there was no corresponding groundswell in favour of revoking laws against female sex workers.

This movement ensured that "prostitution" was associated with trafficking in white women.[6] When the United Nations adopted the law "on the repression and abolition of the trade in human beings and the exploitation of prostitution of others" in 1949, this representation already had strong currency in institutional environments.[7] The paradoxical attitude of feminists with regard to the issue of "prostitution" was to endure. Today, a good number of feminists still advocate for the abolition of sex work while stating their solidarity with sex workers, defined as victims.

A new movement emerged in the West in the 1960s, when some radical feminists defined "prostitution" as the symbol of oppression of women in Western society.[8] In the view of these feminists, women, as a group, are oppressed by men, as a group, but female sex workers are more oppressed than other women. This idea was based first on the distinction between the sexes, contrasting oppressed women with dominating men, and second on the distinction between women in general and "prostitutes," whose oppression was absolute. Thus, radical feminists targeted not the income-producing activities of female sex workers but, rather, the conditions of oppression that both connected them with and separated them from women as a whole.

Radical feminists thus posited "prostitution" as an institution that oppressed women alongside marriage and maternity, as well as rape, sexual harassment, and so on. The concept of oppression was gradually overshadowed by that of victimization and violence; from one to the other was simply a question of degree. In this view, "prostitution" necessarily looked like exploitation, constraint, abuse, and slavery: authors spoke of survival "prostitution," sexual tourism, and sexual slavery (Barry 1982).

Nevertheless, radical feminists wanted to maintain an alliance with their sex worker sisters, and they stood side by side in the fight for decriminalization of sex-work activities.[9] What is more, in keeping with the radical feminist approach, which favours knowledge emerging from the grassroots – that is, women's groups – feminists wanted to listen to the voices of female sex workers. But their focus on the distinction between experience (of "prostitutes") to be listened to and non-experience (of other women) gave way to a focus on the distinction between lucid reasoning (by feminists) and alienated reasoning (by female sex workers) when female sex workers saw themselves as workers and not victims. This approach is reminiscent of the Marxist view that consciousness enlightened by Marxist vision is good consciousness, but that when the proletariat does not conform with the Marxist vision, it suffers from false consciousness.

Thus, the feminist heritage on "prostitution" was also fraught with ambiguities, and it is not surprising that female sex workers and radical feminists were unable to achieve an alliance.

The Debate in the 1980s and '90s

Why Was the Debate Rekindled in Canada in the 1990s?
In the late 1980s and the 1990s, the debate on sex work became internationalized in the wake of globalization of markets and marked expansion of worker migration.[10] At this point, a neo-abolitionist position emerged to promote the elimination of "prostitution" – a contemporary version of the nineteenth-century abolitionist position that advocated the same objective but by applying the laws in a different way.[11] In effect, as noted above, the abolitionists called for criminal laws targeting all facets of the trade and all actors involved, "prostitutes" included. Neo-abolitionists defined female sex workers as victims and wanted to remove them from the criminal justice system. They targeted other actors in these activities, in particular the customers and pimps.[12]

Another position, designating sex work as work and advocating its decriminalization,[13] was held by female sex workers, supported by allies in professional circles (female lawyers, professors, social workers, nurses, and others). A number of neo-abolitionists saw themselves as representative of the *real* feminist vision in this debate. In fact, however, there was no unity in feminist movements and no one had the authority to limit the feminist stance to one or another of these approaches. Furthermore, many proponents of the position of sex work as work identified themselves as feminists.

We shall now examine the arguments and empirical foundations of the two positions.

"Prostitution" as a Form of Violence?

First, we need to understand the meaning of violence in the view of proponents of the concept of sex work as a form of violence. They do not refer to acts of violence against female sex workers, which are more or less common according to the type of activity or the place of work chosen. They state that "prostitution" as such *is* violence. "Prostituted people" are fundamentally victims, as violence is "constitutive of and inherent to prostitution" (Poulin 2004, 51).[14]

Furthermore, globalization forms the background for this definition of the problem. Globalization, in this view, has led to the industrialization and internationalization of the sex trade, so that the industry has become a "fundamental economic power" (Poulin 2004, 127). The sex trade operates through organized crime because "violence is decisive in the production of prostituted people as 'sexual goods'" (Poulin 2004, 129). With the support of economic circles and political powers, criminal networks have seen remarkable growth. Thus, sex work has led to the development of trafficking in women and children, which is controlled by organized crime through the use of terror.

According to Marie-Victoire Louis (1997), "prostitution" forms a system – the prostitutional system – that brings pimps, customers, and sex workers of all ages, mainly women, into contact with each other. This system is the expression of patriarchal systems, which make women sexually dependent, and market systems, which put bodies on the economic market. But, again according to Louis, we must recognize the conceptual specificity of "prostitution" in order to analyze it and compare it to other systems of domination, such as slavery, racism, and capitalism. This approach is also necessary if the intention is to impose an "absolute ban" on "prostitution" and ensure that it no longer corresponds in any way to the "values" of a society or a state (Louis 2006). By abolishing the possibility of market exchange and procuring, one would abolish sex work. However, this would be a major task, as the procuring system now extends across the entire planet in the form of an informal network of criminal organizations of different sizes.

This analysis poses a series of problems, and here we will discuss just a few that we feel are particularly important.

The Figure of the Pimp

In the West, the pimp emerged as a social actor in the field of sex work in the late nineteenth century, when numerous laws were adopted to eliminate "prostitution." The consequence of these changes was to increase the isolation and vulnerability of female sex workers, who then came to depend on the pimp's support and protection (McLaren 1986; Walkowitz 1991).

In the conception of "prostitution" as violence, as we have seen, the pimp occupies a central position and monopolizes the market space. Yet this forced link between the market space and procuring seems to us to be highly problematic. The basis of market exchange involves two social actors: a person who offers services, and another person, a customer, who is willing to purchase them. The pimp is not an essential intermediary. As is the case in a number of jobs, the female sex worker may act independently or choose to work with or for someone.

When we try to verify how systematically pimps are involved in "prostitution" and its corollary, trafficking in women, the empirical data are sorely lacking. Researchers,[15] as well as a number of Canadian commissions of inquiry,[16] have noted the lack of knowledge about these social actors. Indeed, most of the information available is taken from French- and English-language research on the overall operation of a specific form of sex work. The studies informed by a radical feminist approach do not make a distinction between lovers or spouses and working partners, whether they are owners or managers of agencies or establishments or traditional street pimps.[17] In such studies, all of these relationships are associated with exploitation and violence. In contrast, critical research based on the words of female sex workers makes a distinction among managers, exploiters, and lovers or spouses.[18] As there are few empirical data on the management task as such, the stereotype of the pimp as the perfect villain of the sex industry is rarely challenged.

One thing is certain: the idea that pimps are omnipresent in the sex industry does not seem very credible given the research available. In the 1980s, research on "prostitution" in Canada commissioned by the Fraser Committee revealed the presence of pimps in street "prostitution" in some Canadian cities, but not in others. For example, in research on "prostitution" in the Maritimes, Nikita Cook (1984) devoted a section to pimps in Halifax but noted that they were absent from other cities in the region. More recent research by Frances Shaver (1993) on street "prostitution" in Montreal found that the majority of people worked alone. In the research that we have conducted since 2002 on street sex work in the Ottawa-Gatineau region and in erotic establishments in the Montreal and Toronto regions (Parent and Bruckert 2005, 2006), some female participants talked about managers, but we found almost no evidence of exploitative, violent pimps. Furthermore, in more than forty interviews conducted with male and female escorts in the Montreal, Toronto, and Ottawa regions,[19] we found that these workers were acting autonomously. Thus, the available empirical data indicate, at the very least, that the presence of pimps may vary widely depending on the sector and the context.

Thus, given the scarcity of the data available, it is hard to understand the claim that 85 to 90 percent of female sex workers are under the authority of a pimp. Yet this is what Poulin (2004, 158) states, referring to five pieces of empirical research conducted by different researchers between 1982 and 2002. These results do not reveal much about the phenomenon, and given the state of current knowledge, no researcher can dispense with subjecting his or her hypotheses on the importance and the role of the pimp in sex work to the proof of empirical verifications. This step is even more important when it is claimed that pimps play a pivotal role in what proponents of the neo-abolitionist approach call the prostitutional system.

When we consider the methods chosen by the neo-abolitionists to support their position, other problems emerge. We examine below the neo-abolitionists' use of statistics, their arguments for challenging the distinction between voluntary and non-voluntary "prostitution," and the call for the right not to prostitute oneself.

The Use of Statistics

A number of neo-abolitionists place great emphasis on statistics to buttress their arguments. However, they do not make critical use of these statistics, even though this is essential to any scientific approach. Take, for example, the following excerpt from *La mondialisation des industries du sexe*:

> Every year, about 500,000 female victims of trafficking for the purpose
> of prostitution are put on the sexual venality market in the fifteen
> countries of the EU; 75 percent of female victims of such trafficking
> are twenty-five years of age or younger, and an indeterminate but
> very high proportion of them are minors. About four million women
> and children are victims of the global prostitution trade each year.
> (Poulin 2004, 66, our translation)

The reference, the European Parliament's Commission des droits de la
femme et de l'égalité des chances (2003), is given in a footnote. When we
check this source, we find that it refers not to a report or a research publication, but to a communication to members. Thus, the basis for the
statistics presented is not known. We must either believe the author who
presented them or dig to find the complete reference. We can only presume that all the figures presented are from the same source, since no
further information is supplied. In any case, it is open to question how
it was possible to quantify a largely clandestine phenomenon in countries
in which the collection and quality of statistics are highly variable.

Furthermore, in a quarterly newsletter published in April 2001, the
International Organization for Migration (Organisation internationale
pour les migrations 2001) acknowledged that statistics on the scope of
trafficking were limited and the calculations used to produce them were
unclear. Several hypotheses were proposed to explain this: the illegal
and hidden nature of trafficking; the absence of anti-trafficking legislation in a number of countries; victims' refusal to cooperate with the
authorities; and the absence of statistics and lack of interest in conducting research on the issue.

A number of national and international organizations charged with
fighting human trafficking nevertheless employ statistics to highlight
the scope of the phenomenon that they are denouncing. For example,
in 2000, the National Organization for Women (NOW) estimated that
50,000 women and children were victims of trafficking for the purpose
of "prostitution" every year in the United States (Chapkis 2005, 53). This
figure was in fact taken from a document by Amy O'Neill Richard
(1999, 3), who estimated that between 45,000 and 50,000 women and

children were trafficked in the United States to become workers in sweatshops, domestic workers, farm workers, or "prostitutes" (Chapkis 2005). This statistic, an approximation to begin with, does not cover exclusively the phenomenon targeted by NOW: trafficking in women and children for the purpose of "prostitution." It is therefore meaningless. Furthermore, the figures given by O'Neill Richard,[20] and then used by NOW and critiqued by Wendy Chapkis (2005), are a good reflection of the potential trajectory of a statistic accepted as truth in societies in which figures have probative power.

The Lack of Distinction between Voluntary and Involuntary "Prostitution"
Although the neo-abolitionists depend heavily on statistics to document the scope of activities in the sex industry, they have not paid much attention to the diversified speech of female sex workers in an attempt to understand the phenomenon. They posit, simply, that "prostitution" is violence, and they question the distinction between "voluntary prostitution" and "forced prostitution." There thus cannot be sex work as such; rather, "prostitution" is simply a manifestation of domination, just like slavery, colonialism, and other such activities. However, although they leave out the plural voices of female sex workers on the grounds that they are alienated, the neo-abolitionists nevertheless propose explanatory scenarios for these workers' powerlessness that challenge the distinction between "voluntary prostitution" and "forced prostitution."

For instance, Poulin (2004, 149) offers an analysis of the commodification of female sex workers, who, he posits, are sold to successive networks of pimps and to customers. In Poulin's view, this process involves not only trafficking in individuals, but casting these individuals as merchandise through both the influence of the pimps and the life history of women as victims. According to this analysis, "prostitutes," who are the property of pimps, are dehumanized and objectified. After ensuring that they will become submissive by orchestrating sessions of rape, torture, and so on, the pimps retain their hold over their victims by the systematic use of violence. Thus, the "prostitutes" bring their pimps enormous profits.

But to understand why certain people choose to sell sexual services one must also examine their life history. Women who opt for "prostitution," in the neo-abolitionist view, will have had a past marked by abuse and repeated physical and sexual violence. Thus one could not say that they had a choice. Much empirical research[21] conducted over several decades has established a correlation between these forms of victimization and "prostitution," but a correlation is not a causal link, and there is a lack of empirical research demonstrating that physical and sexual abuse is decisive in understanding the choices of all people who opt for sex work.

In Shaver's (1993) view, the idea that being a victim of abuse in the past leads to "prostitution" is a myth rather than a scientific hypothesis. When we take as a point of departure a comparison between female sex workers and a control group, the weakness of this hypothesis emerges clearly. Shaver (1993) consulted a series of research papers on sex work.[22] She observed that a large proportion of the female sex workers interviewed reported having been childhood victims of physical and sexual violence. In Quebec, for example, 44 percent of the interviewees stated that they had been forced to have sexual relations with one or more family members (Shaver 1993, 159). But according to the results of a national survey conducted for the Badgley Committee (1984), 53.5 percent of women and 22.3 percent of men indicated that they had been victims of undesired sexual acts in the past. The category "undesired sexual act" used in the survey was broad and included both relatively benign and reprehensible behaviours, but the research on male and female sex workers did not offer details on the type of abuse suffered. In fact, sexual abuse in childhood is not all that rare; in Canada, one woman in two has experienced sexual abuse before reaching adult age, according to the Badgley Committee survey (Shaver 1993, 160). Thus, although the hypothesis that associates the history of women's lives and being forced into "prostitution" supports the neo-abolitionist theory, it is not based on any solid empirical data.[23]

The Right of Women Not to Prostitute Themselves

Finally, in the approach that defines "prostitution" as violence, the objective is to make sure that it is wiped out. Paradoxically, this objective is based on the right of women to control their bodies (Louis 1991). In contemporary Western society, feminist women's groups have demanded the right to control their bodies and, among other things, the abolition of laws that criminalize abortion. They have campaigned for the right to free choice. And they have obtained this right, which involves an alternative, and are thus holders of a right in the full sense: I have complete authority to control my body and I can choose to have an abortion or not.[24]

However, Louis (1991) refers not to the right to control one's body but to the duty to protect one's body, symbolized, in her view, exclusively by the female body. In fact, she demands that the community have the right to ban "prostitution" and reintroduces the stranglehold of a superior authority over the right of women to control their bodies. In this case, it would be not a political, legal, or religious authority that holds legitimate power over women's bodies, but the feminist definition of the oppression of women. Each woman thus has not a right to control her body but an individual duty to protect her body against "prostitution," conceived as violence. Louis feels that this is necessary in order to "break down ... the ideology according to which a woman receives value and life because she belongs to a man" (Louis 1991, our translation). In this sense, it is the patriarchal system that must be attacked. But we may also wonder why Louis did not include marriage in her recommendations or propose the right not to marry – marriage being the patriarchal institution par excellence.

"Prostitution" as a Form of Sex Work?

In the mid-1970s, groups of female sex workers demanded recognition of "prostitution" as a form of work.[25] Subsequently, a new empirical and theoretical view of sex work emerged in criminology and sociology.[26] Benefiting in part from feminist contributions, this perspective changes the approach to the phenomenon. It looks at sex work by distinguishing between recognized and unrecognized work, identifying obstacles to social recognition of sex work, focusing in a new way on the issue of trafficking in women for the purpose of "prostitution," and exploring the limits of the traditional distinctions among work, sexuality, and privacy.

An Unrecognized Form of Work

This perspective explores the social implications of recognized work and, thus, of unrecognized work.[27] A social role such as the trade of hairdresser, for example, involves a certain number of rules that are imposed on or guide the behaviours of individuals. A hairdresser establishes a relationship with a customer who expects a certain reception and services that respect certain rules – essentially, offering the services of cutting, dyeing, and curling hair. The hairdresser must be polite and attentive to the customer's needs. There is no question, at least in principle, of exploring new avenues without the customer's approval. The two actors share these general expectations even at their first meeting. The established rules are not limited to the individuals directly concerned but are socially inscribed. The individuals may develop certain specific aspects of their interaction, but these will not affect, essentially, the content of the hairdresser's work. The professional thus does not have unlimited freedom in offering services, and the customer, in turn, cannot make absolutely any demand. Each must respect the rules of their respective roles in this interaction. The refusal to conform with these roles may lead to different types of sanctions imposed by the client on the professional, and vice versa.

But sex work, which is unrecognized work, does not offer a stabilized normative framework to regulate interactions and define the rules for exchanges between customers and female sex workers. For these workers, different questions remain open. What services does the customer expect? What is the appropriate way to present them? Will the customer be problematic from the point of view of safety? In turn, the customer will wonder what services he can expect, how to ask for them, what the worker's qualifications are, what level of closeness to establish with her, and so on.

Of course, with experience, the worker learns a series of rules specific to the trade or to her sector (massage parlours and so on) in a given neighbourhood. She cannot, however, either presume that everyone is familiar with these rules or base her working methods on norms that are socially recognized as legitimate.

Obstacles to Social Recognition of Sex Work

In this context, what are the obstacles to sex work being accepted as work and thus being socially recognized? Above all, how can it be seen as a concrete form of work that is not socially "excluded"?

First, laws banning a number of activities associated with sex work make it impossible to recognize it as work. But beyond this legal interdiction, there is generally a moral judgment that serves as a point of departure for defining "prostitution." For instance, if an observer conceives of sex work first and foremost as a form of unjust exploitation, slavery, or violence, independent of the empirical data (working conditions, remuneration, and so on), that observer can only condemn it morally and refuse to consider it a form of work.

Let us see what happens when an observer does not distinguish between *slavery* and the *sale of sexual services*. This observer represents all forms of sale of sexual services as instances of slavery. Yet a slave is a person from whom one can require anything at all. One can ask this person to offer sexual services, embroider tablecloths, wash floors – in short, to obey any order at any time. If we regard sex work as a form of slavery, we must thus include in the notion of slavery paid activities by a free adult woman who sells sexual services. In this context, slavery is likened to freely chosen work, and it becomes very difficult to distinguish them from each other. The female sex worker may be considered merchandise and the customer an exploiter. Having contaminated the concepts of both slavery and work, we can no longer observe what is occurring empirically, but only argue based on emotions and value judgments.

More concretely, from this position we can no longer observe other aspects of the interpersonal relationship between the female sex worker and the customer (various emotional connections, reciprocal assistance, completely respectful and professional relationship, and so on). Nor can we consider relevant an analysis of how the work is organized, the risks of the trade, and so on.[28] It is thus understandable that this type of observation provokes a reaction from female sex workers who do not consider themselves as slaves or as pawns in the power relations that may exist between them and the manager or the customer. They consider themselves citizens whose rights should be respected, and they do not see themselves as merchandise simply because their paid activities offend an observer's sense of morality.[29] This observer, in contrast, constrained to a point of view that allows only the concept of slavery, remains deaf to the workers' voices and accuses them of being blind.

The same reasoning applies to other blurred conceptual lines, such as those between "violence" and "prostitution," as seen above. If we link the two concepts by stating that "prostitution" is violence, then all of the female sex worker's activities – her relations with both customers and managers – are categorized as violence. We can thus no longer distinguish specific situations as violent or search for solutions; everything is violence. Yet, if one is violent toward a worker, that worker's paid activities are nonetheless work and not simply the fruit of violence. It is the same for the female sex worker, whose trade, like so many other occupations, involves risks.

This distinction between work and violence has led a number of researchers to observe the risks of the trade and the defence strategies and mechanisms deployed to counter them or neutralize their consequences. These researchers have considered the violence perpetrated by aggressors, pimps, and the public, as well as between colleagues, and they have also brought to light the violence perpetrated by the controlling forces against sex workers. This underlies their analysis of how laws and their application affect the risks associated with sex work.[30]

A New Look at Trafficking in Women for the Purpose of "Prostitution"[31]

The association between trafficking in women and "prostitution" has also come within the purview of the new approach, the proponents of which have shown that sex work is one of the forms of work available to many women in third-world countries affected by globalization.[32] Those who travel to a new destination are among the general flow of migrant workers. We can thus observe the phenomenon from the point of view of the distinction between legal and illegal migrant labour.

When we look at illegal migrant labour, we can establish yet another distinction. On the one hand, when a worker can travel unconstrained, she is part of the general migratory flow; on the other hand, if she is coerced or kidnapped, the notion of trafficking is used. In the latter case, when the migrant worker arrives at her destination, she may or may not be subjected to working conditions that are abusive, or even akin to slavery.

It should be noted that in privileging the distinction between legal and illegal migrant labour, we emphasize the vulnerability of the worker independent of the type of work that she is involved in. We also avoid the trap of moral judgment with regard to sex work. Jo Doezema (1998) has clearly described the risks associated with establishing a dichotomy between voluntary and involuntary "prostitution." If a worker agrees to migrate to work in the sex work sector, she is responsible for the poor working conditions that are imposed on her. She's the bad victim, who should have known better. If, however, the worker agrees to migrate to perform domestic work, but when she arrives at her destination she is subjected to unacceptable working conditions, she does not have to have been misled with regard to her work plans to be considered a victim.

In the model of sex work as a trade, female sex workers are defined as people capable of choice and action and not as victims. Just like other workers, they have many different profiles, ranging from white and Western to racialized to having origins in developing countries. It goes without saying that different groups of women may have different attitudes toward their work. Some define themselves as professionals and feel that their work offers the possibility of an exciting career.[33] It seems, however, that the majority consider sex work to be one option among others on a limited list of more or less interesting jobs.[34] It is obvious that the "choices" are, to begin with, limited by widely variable opportunities. I could become a psychologist because I failed the entrance exams for medical school; I could become a secretary because I wasn't accepted into an art program. All over the world, women choose sex work, according to Amalia Lucia Cabezas (1998, 84), for "the same reasons why most people who work in boring, hazardous and exploitative jobs" choose to do so.

The Distinction among Work, Sexuality, and Intimacy

Finally, considering sex work to be a form of work runs contrary to the general notion that sexuality should not be part of work because it may disrupt the work environment and impede profit making. But if we look more closely, we realize that many jobs include tasks with some sexual dimensions. For example, in a study in the hotel sector, using a sample of men and women assigned to customer service in a bar (waitresses and bartender), Lisa Adkins (1992) observed that employers had specific criteria for women they hired that contributed to sexualizing their work. They required the female workers to be attractive (appropriate physique and clothing) and to be charming and flirtatious in their exchanges with customers. They did not have the same expectations of their male employees. This dimension of work may be overlooked because it is not mentioned at the top of the list of services offered.

Moreover, we challenge sex work by saying that it transgresses the boundaries between public and private life, between work and intimacy. It therefore must be harmful to individuals. But managing these boundaries, independent of the type of work, is part of everyday life.

We know, for example, that work-related stress can affect relations with family and friends, and that jobs requiring long hours or involving frequent or prolonged travel can have an impact on private life. Certain professions expose workers to conditions of intimacy with customers or collaborators: this may be the case for physicians, fashion photographers, and especially theatre and movie actors, who may be called upon to play intimate scenes that include sexual contact. However, no one thinks of discrediting these forms of work.

Observing "prostitution" as a form of work, we can compare its component activities with those in other service-sector jobs. And if we recognize that there may be a sexual dimension in different forms of work, we can compare sex work to the work of a nurse, for example, or to that of a psychologist, a physician, or other professionals. Thus, we realize that the sexual dimension is generally hidden. We suffer from tunnel vision in two senses: on the one hand, we do not see the sexual dimension in other jobs; on the other hand, we see sex work only through the prism of sexuality (Parent and Bruckert 2005).

If sex work is considered a form of work, avenues are opened for research and analysis. This way, the complexity of the issues is not glossed over, and the voice of female sex workers is not discredited. Some state that they enjoy their work; others consider it a lesser evil or describe it as a very difficult experience. In this respect, they are like many female workers in a number of trades, and there is no need to deny their point of view – to accuse them of false consciousness – to maintain the scientific pertinence of this approach.

Conclusion

The current debate over sex work is challenging in more than one regard. First, it is strangely reminiscent of the late-nineteenth-century debate discussed above and reveals how much, even today, this topic reflects moral positions, whether conservative, religious, or feminist. Second, proponents of the conception of "prostitution" as a form of violence base their position on arguments that appear scientific, but the foundations of this position are highly debatable – even though, without verification, they may seem convincing. Finally, although the voices of female sex workers were, in effect, inaudible in the nineteenth century, today they are too often discredited under the pretext of their alienation. And in all cases, sex workers pay the price for this controversy. In the meantime, there is no concern about the fate of many female workers all over the world, in the sex industry and in other sectors, who work under abusive conditions and whose rights are flouted.

Notes

This chapter was produced on the basis of previously published texts, including Parent and Bruckert (2005, 2007). Readers will find some arguments presented in greater detail in these other publications.

1 See Backhouse (1985), Lévesque (1995), and McLaren (1986). It should be noted that Canada, following the lead of England, adopted the *Contagious Disease Act* in 1865, but this statute was never applied and was not renewed at the end of its five-year validity period.
2 See McLaren (1986), 140-41.
3 See also Chapter 2 of this book.
4 See Dubois and Gordon (1983) and Walkowitz (1991), who examine British feminists' involvement with this issue during the nineteenth century.
5 As were all women of the period.
6 See also Chapter 5 of this book.
7 Doezema (2000).
8 See, among others, Barry (1982) and Millett (1972).

9 Some were in favour of decriminalization as such; others were in favour of the adoption of regulations to better protect the workers. On this subject, see Coderre and Parent (2001).

10 See, among others, Toupin (2002).

11 See, among others, Audet (2005), Geadah (2003), Jeffreys (1999), Louis (1997), Poulin (2004), and Raymond (2004).

12 See Chapter 2 of this book.

13 See, among others, Kempadoo and Doezema (1998), Parent and Bruckert (2006), and Pheterson (1989).

14 In this section, we draw mainly on the work of Richard Poulin, an important figure in the current debate in Quebec and French Canada. All translations of quotations from his 2004 work in this chapter are ours.

15 See, among others, Lowman (2001) and Weitzer (2005).

16 This issue surfaced in four Canadian committees charged with studying prostitution in the country: the Badgley Committee (1984), the Fraser Committee (1985), the Federal/Provincial/Territorial Working Group (1998), and the Subcommittee on Solicitation Laws (2006).

17 See, among others, Parker (2004).

18 See, among others, Jeffrey and McDonald (2006).

19 This research was funded by the Social Sciences and Humanities Research Council.

20 We consulted O'Neill Richard's (1999) report directly.

21 One can get a good idea of the amount of research by accessing a databank such as *Criminal Justice Abstracts*. We did so on 26 October 2009, and the keywords "prostitution" and "abuse" brought up 288 sources, including books and articles.

22 Shaver used data from ten pieces of empirical research commissioned by the Department of Justice Canada and her own research, including an empirical study involving eighty interviews.

23 See also Nadon, Koverola, and Schludermann (1998).

24 See, among others, Lamoureux (1983, 1993).

25 See Chapters 3 and 4 of this book.

26 See, among others, Coderre and Parent (2001), Parent (1994, 2001), Parent and Bruckert (2005), and Shaver (1993).

27 See Dahrendorf's (1973) analysis of social roles.

28 Thus, we should not be surprised at the absence of such dimensions in publications by Audet (2005), Geadah (2003), and Poulin (2004), to cite just a few authors.

29 See, among others, Kempadoo and Doezema (1998).

30 See, among others, Parent and Bruckert (2005).

31 See also Chapter 5 of this book.

32 See, among others, Kempadoo and Doezema (1998).

33 See, among others, Chapkis (1997), Monet (2005).

34 See, among others, Carthonnet (2003).

References

Adkins, Lisa. 1992. Sexual Work and the Employment of Women in the Service Industries. In *Gender and Bureaucracy*, ed. Mike Savage and Anne Witz, 207-28. Oxford: Blackwell.

Audet, Élaine. 2005. *Prostitution. Perspectives féministes*. Montreal: Sisyphe.

Backhouse, Constance. 1985. Nineteenth-century Canadian Prostitution Law: Reflection of a Discriminatory Society. *Histoire sociale* 18 (36): 387-423.

Badgley Committee. 1984. *Report of the Committee on Sexual Offences against Children and Youth*. Ottawa: Supply and Services Canada.

Barry, Kathleen. 1982. *L'esclavage sexuel de la femme*. Paris: Stock.

Cabezas, Amalia Lucia. 1998. Discourses on Prostitution: The Case of Cuba. In *Global Sex Workers: Rights, Resistance, and Redefinition*, ed. Kamala Kempadoo and Jo Doezema, 79-86. New York: Routledge.

Carthonnet, Claire. 2003. *J'ai des choses à vous dire. Une prostituée témoigne*. Paris: Robert Laffont.

Chapkis, Wendy. 1997. *Live Sex Acts*. New York: Routledge.

–. 2005. Soft Glove, Punishing Fist: The Trafficking Victims Protection Act of 2000. In *Regulating Sex: The Politics of Intimacy and Identity*, ed. Elizabeth Bernstein and Laurie Schaffner, 51-66. New York: Routledge.

Coderre, Cécile, and Colette Parent. 2001. Le Deuxième Sexe et la prostitution: pour repenser la problématique dans une perspective féministe. In *Le Deuxième Sexe, une relecture en trois temps, 1949-1971-1999*, ed. Cécile Coderre et Marie-Blanche Tahon, 73-89. Montreal: Les éditions du remue-ménage.

Commission des droits de la femme et de l'égalité des chances. 2003. *Communications aux membres*. Objet: principales activités au cours de la cinquième législature, Parlement européen, Direction générale des commissions et délégations, 25 September, CM/505949FR.doc., PE 331.5/rev.

Cook, Nikita. 1984. *Documents de travail sur la pornographie et la prostitution, rapport nº 12, Rapport sur la prostitution dans les Maritimes*. Ottawa: Gouvernement du Canada, Ministère de la Justice, Direction de la politique, des programmes et de la recherche, section de la recherche et de la statistique.

Dahrendorf, Ralf. 1973. *Homo Sociologicus*. London: Routledge and Kegan Paul.

Doezema, Jo. 1998. Forced to Choose: Beyond the Voluntary versus Forced Prostitution Dichotomy. In *Global Sex Workers: Rights, Resistance, and Redefinition*, ed. Kamala Kempadoo and Jo Doezema, 34-49. New York: Routledge.

–. 2000. Loose Women or Lost Women? The Reemergence of the Myth of "White Slavery" in Contemporary Discourses of "Trafficking in Women." *Gender Issues* 18 (1): 23-50.

Dubois, Ellen Carol, and Linda Gordon. 1983. Seeking Ecstasy on the Battlefield: Danger and Pleasure in Nineteenth-century Feminist Sexual Thought. *Feminist Studies* 9 (1): 7-25.

Federal/Provincial/Territorial Working Group on Prostitution. 1998. *Report and Recommendations in Respect of Legislation, Policy and Practices Concerning Prostitution-Related Activities.* Ottawa: Department of Justice Canada.

Geadah, Yolande. 2003. *La prostitution. Un métier comme un autre?* Montreal: VLB.

Jeffrey, Leslie Ann, and Gayle McDonald. 2006. *Sex Workers in the Maritimes Talk Back.* Vancouver: UBC Press.

Jeffreys, Sheila. 1999. Globalizing Sexual Exploitation: Sex Tourism and the Traffic of Women. *Leisure Studies* 18, 179-96.

Kempadoo, Kamala, and Jo Doezema, eds. 1998. *Global Sex Workers: Rights, Resistance, and Redefinition.* New York: Routledge.

Lamoureux, Diane. 1983. La lutte pour le droit à l'avortement (1969-81). *Revue d'histoire de l'Amérique française* 37 (1): 81-90.

Lamoureux, Diane, ed. 1993. *Avortement: pratiques, enjeux, contrôle social.* Montreal: Les éditions du remue-ménage.

Lévesque, Andrée. 1995. *Résistance et transgression. Études en histoire des femmes au Québec.* Montreal: Les éditions du remue-ménage.

Louis, Marie-Victoire. 1991. Prostitution et droits de la personne. *Cette violence dont nous ne voulons plus* 11/12: 3-10, www.marievictoirelouis.net.

–. 1997. L'ONU, les gouvernements et le proxénétisme. De la conférence de Nairobi (1985) à la conférence de Pékin (1995), Le corps humain est-il devenu un objet d'échange sur le marché mondial? www.marievictoirelouis.net/document.php?id=503&themeid=336.

–. 2006. Interview par Grégoire Téry, À propos des rapports entre "la traite des êtres humains" et le proxénétisme. www.marievictoirelouis.net/document.php?id=525&themeid=336.

Lowman, John. 2001. *Identifying Research Gaps in the Prostitution Literature.* Ottawa: Research and Statistics Division, Department of Justice Canada.

McLaren, John. 1986. Chasing the Social Evil: Moral Fervour and the Evolution of Canada's Prostitution Laws, 1867-1917. *Canadian Journal of Law and Society* 1: 125-65.

Millett, Kate. 1972. *La prostitution. Quatuor pour voix féminines.* Paris: Denoël/Gonthier.

Monet, Veronica. 2005. College Graduate Makes Good as a Courtesan. In *Sex Workers Write a Changing Industry,* ed. Annie Oakley, 124-37. Emeryville, CA: Seal Press.

Nadon, Susan M., Catherine Koverola, and Eduard H. Schludermann. 1998. Antecedents to Prostitution: Childhood Victimization. *Journal of Interpersonal Violence* 13 (2): 206-21.

National Organization for Women (NOW). 2000. *Legislative Update, 12 June,* http://www.now.org/issues/legislat/06-12-2000.htm.

O'Neill Richard, Amy. 1999. *International Trafficking in Women to the United States: A Contemporary Manifestation of Slavery and Organized Crime.* Washington, DC: Center for the Study of Intelligence, CIA, sciencestage.com/d/1328917/international

-trafficking-in-women-to-the-united-states-a-contemporarymanifestation-of
-slavery-and-organized-crime.html.

Organisation internationale pour les migrations (OIM). 2001. Les nouveaux chiffres de l'OIM sur l'ampleur mondiale de la traite. *Traite des migrants,* quarterly bulletin, special issue, www.iom.int.

Parent, Colette. 1994. La "prostitution" ou le commerce des services sexuels. In *Traité de problèmes sociaux,* ed. Simon Langlois, Yves Martin, and Fernand Dumont, 393-407. Quebec City: Institut québécois de recherche sur la culture.

–. 2001. Les identités sexuelles et les travailleuses de l'industrie du sexe à l'aube du nouveau millénaire. *Sociologie et Société* 33 (1): 159-78.

Parent, Colette, and Chris Bruckert. 2005. Le travail du sexe dans les établissements de services érotiques: une forme de travail marginalisé. *Déviance et Société* 29 (1): 33-54.

–. 2006. Répondre aux besoins des travailleuses du sexe de rue: un objectif qui passe par la décriminalisation de leurs activités de travail. *Reflets* 11: 112-45.

–. 2007. Le travail du sexe: oppression ou travail? In *Problèmes sociaux* 4, ed. Henri Dorvil, 119-45. Quebec City: Presses de l'Université du Québec.

Parker, Joe. 2004. Understanding Systems of Prostitution. In *Not For Sale: Feminists Resisting Prostitution and Pornography,* ed. Christine Stark and Rebecca Whisnant, 7-10. North Melbourne: Spinifex Press.

Pheterson, Gail. 1989. *A Vindication of the Rights of Whores.* Seattle: Seal Press.

Poulin, Richard. 2004. *La mondialisation des industries du sexe. Prostitution, pornographie, traite des femmes et des enfants.* Ottawa: L'interligne.

Raymond, Janice G. 2004. Prostitution on Demand: Legalizing the Buyers as Sexual Consumers. *Violence Against Women* 10 (10): 1156-86.

Shaver, Frances. 1993. Prostitution: A Female Crime? In *In Conflict with the Law: Women and the Canadian Justice System,* ed. Ellen Alderberg and Claudia Currie, 153-73. Vancouver: Press Gang Publishers.

Special Committee on Pornography and Prostitution (Fraser Committee). 1985. *Report of the Special Committee on Pornography and Prostitution.* Ottawa: Supply and Services Canada.

Subcommittee on Solicitation Laws of the House of Commons. 2006. *The Challenge of Change: A Study of Canada's Criminal Prostitution Laws.* Ottawa: House of Commons.

Toupin, Louise. 2002. La scission politique du féminisme international sur la question du "trafic des femmes": vers la "migration" d'un certain féminisme radical? *Recherches féministes* 15 (2): 9-40.

Walkowitz, Judith R. 1991. Sexualités dangereuses. In *Histoires des femmes en Occident, Le xixe siècle,* ed. George Duby, Michelle Perrot, and Geneviève Fraisse, 389-418. Paris: Plon.

Weitzer, Ronald. 2005. New Directions in Research on Prostitution. *Crime, Law and Social Change* 43 (4-5): 211-35.

Regulating Sex Work

Between Victimization and Freedom to Choose

PATRICE CORRIVEAU

2

Is "Prostitution" Illegal in Canada?

Contrary to what most Canadians think, adult "prostitution" has never been illegal in Canada. In fact, the first *Criminal Code of Canada* (1892) did not interdict the sale of sexual services by consenting adults. However, paradoxically, a number of provisions of the *Criminal Code* blocked (and still block) the free practice of "prostitution" – that is, in our terms, sex work. The statutes in effect in the nineteenth century to fight against vagrancy, procuring, and whorehouses were probative examples of criminal laws aimed at controlling activities linked to "prostitution." However, history shows that these laws essentially targeted "female prostitutes." For example, according to section 175(1)(c), on vagrancy, a vagrant was "a common prostitute or nightwalker"; the pronoun "herself" used in the section made it clear that the definition applied exclusively to women. Indeed, the statute mandated the arrest of women upon simple suspicion of being "prostitutes." Because these "nightwalkers" occupied the public space, they somehow transgressed the separation between private and public space in "normal" society.

The legal provision on vagrancy thus made street "prostitution" an infraction based essentially on the public presence of women and not on the act of selling or offering sexual services. Not until 1972 was it struck down and replaced by section 195.1 on solicitation in a public place, which displaced the illegality from the person to her behaviour (see the *Criminal Law Amendment Act*, 1972, S.C., ch. 12, s. 15). Now, "Every person who solicits any person in a public place for the purpose of prostitution" was guilty of an offence.[1] However, a ruling made by the Supreme Court of Canada in 1978 limited the provision's scope. The court opined that for there to be solicitation, there had to be proof of pressure or insistence by the accused; this insistence (or pressure) also had to be directed toward one client in particular and not consist of a series of advances toward potential customers.[2] Deeming it impossible to control nuisances related to "prostitution" with this legal tool, police representatives and a number of municipalities and residents' groups lobbied legislators to change the law.

The legislature gave in to this pressure in 1984 by creating the Special Committee on Pornography and Prostitution (the Fraser Committee), which recommended that section 195.1 on solicitation be abrogated but that it be illegal if a person "stands, stops, wanders about in or drives through a public place for purposes of offering to engage in prostitution" (Fraser Committee 1985, 684). As the authors of the report noted, "It is not our intention to criminalize street soliciting per se ... The problem is the *nuisance* created by some prostitutes, some customers, and sightseers, in any location which becomes a regular site of prostitution activity" (Fraser Committee 1985, 661; emphasis added). The Fraser Committee was also in favour of partial decriminalization of "prostitution," notably with regard to "prostitution establishments." It concluded that both legislative and social reforms would have to be instituted to respond to the "prostitution" problem.

Setting aside the Fraser Committee's recommendations, the Canadian legislature adopted Bill C-49, *An Act to Amend the Criminal Code (Prostitution)*, replacing section 195.1 of the *Criminal Code* on solicitation with a law aiming to control street "prostitution" more effectively. According to the minister of justice at the time, Mark MacGuigan, this statute would attack only the nuisance created by street solicitation – that is, it would criminalize *public activities* related to the sale of sexual services. This section – section 213 of the current *Criminal Code* – also makes it an offence to *communicate* with or try to stop a person in a public place with the goal of obtaining or offering sexual services. As we shall see below, not only has this new legal provision not succeeded in reducing street "prostitution" activities, but it makes female sex workers more vulnerable to abuse by customers and to the discretionary power of the police. Yet, in May 1990, the Supreme Court of Canada ruled that the provisions of section 213 of the *Criminal Code* related to communication constituted a reasonable and appropriate measure for wiping out a social nuisance.

In March 2012, in *Canada v. Bedford* (2012 ONCA 186), three of the five justices of the Court of Appeal for Ontario also considered "that the communicating provision in s. 213(1)(c) does not offend the principles of fundamental justice. Accordingly, it does not infringe the respondents' s. 7 Charter rights." Nevertheless, the justices unanimously opined "that ss. 210 and 212(1)(j) of the *Criminal Code* are unconstitutional" (2012 ONCA 186, 131) because they prevent female sex workers from working freely under safe conditions.

Yet, as we will see, the two dissenting judges of the Court of Appeal for Ontario, following the example of Judge Himel of the Superior Court of Ontario (2010 ONSC 4264), felt that ample evidence had been presented to the court that street female sex workers are highly exposed to violence and that section 213 on communication interferes with their safety. Based on the conclusions of Judge Himel and evidence presented in court, the dissenting justices of the Court of Appeal also felt that prostitutes, "particularly those who work on the street, are at high risk of being the victims of physical violence and that the communicating provision places street prostitutes at greater risk of experiencing violence" (2012 ONCA 186, 134). They concluded, "The affidavit evidence in this case provides critical insight into the experience and knowledge of people who have worked on the streets, and who have been exposed to the risk of violence first-hand. This type of evidence should not be set aside lightly. The trial judge had a firm basis on which to find that the communicating provision endangers prostitutes by denying them the opportunity to screen clients" (2012 ONCA 186, 139).

When "Prostitution" Upsets Public Morality

The Repressive Model in Force in Canada

To regulate "prostitution," Canada has thus opted for a "repressive" – also called prohibitionist – system, which aims for nothing less than eradication of the types of activities that upset the public morality.[3] The countries that advocate such a model accept "prostitution" as neither a trade nor a behaviour. Based on the *Convention for the Suppression of the Traffic in Persons and the Exploitation of the Prostitution of Others*, written in 1949 – and not on the recommendations of the fourth World Conference on Women in 1995, which, implicitly and rightly, distinguished forced from voluntary "prostitution" – these countries deem that "prostitution" goes against human dignity and must be eliminated by any means necessary, including suppression (United Nations 1995; see also Chapter 5 of this book). To reach this goal, a number of European countries (France, Italy, Spain, Portugal, Denmark, and others), as well as the United States and Canada, chose to criminalize not "prostitution" in itself but everything that makes it possible to practise sex work, such as solicitation on public roads, procuring, and brothels.

Thus, paradoxically, without officially banning "prostitution" in the *Criminal Code*, Canada penalizes the four main activities associated with it. In other words, it is still almost impossible to legally practise sex work in Canada even though it is not illegal to sell or purchase sexual services.[4] Indeed, section 213, as we have just seen, forbids *communication* in a public place to offer or obtain sexual services, and section 210 bans *keeping or living in a bawdy-house*. According to the definition in the *Criminal Code*, a "bawdy-house" – or brothel – is any location (hotel, house, apartment, parking lot) used for the purpose of "prostitution" (or for performing indecent acts as defined by the law). The Canadian courts, however, have emphasized that to be found guilty under section 210, a person has to be at the location for illicit purposes, and not by mistake. Similarly, section 211 makes it an offence to *take or transport* a person to a brothel. To be found guilty, the defendant has to be aware that he was going to a bawdy-house.

Finally, section 212 represses *procuring* and living on the avails of "prostitution." This section has so broad a scope that it can, in principle, apply to anyone living with a female sex worker. In fact, this criticism was made by the Fraser Committee, which commented that "in the *Criminal Code* provisions dealing with exploitative conduct ... the concern of the criminal law *should be confined to conduct which is violent or which threatens force*" (1985, 537; emphasis added). However, unlike communication, for which the prosecution is tasked with proving that it took place, under section 212, to "procure" and "attempt to procure" "do not require evidence of pressure or immediate insistence."[5] In addition, páragraph 212(1)(j) stipulates that the accused must prove that he or she is not living on the avails of his or her spouse or co-renter, for example. In effect, according to the *Criminal Code*, "Evidence that a person lives with or is habitually in the company of a prostitute or lives in a common bawdy-house is, *in the absence of evidence to the contrary*, proof that the person lives on the avails of prostitution" (section 212 (3); emphasis added). The March 2012 ruling by the Court of Appeal for Ontario, which declared sections 210 and 212 of the *Criminal Code* unconstitutional, will be a game changer in years to come. At the time of writing, however, it is impossible to know what form the legislative changes will take, especially because it is very possible that the federal government will appeal the Ontario court's ruling to the Supreme Court of Canada.

Why Does This Repressive Model Harm Female Sex Workers?

As the Canadian HIV/AIDS Legal Network (2005, 18) broadly suggests, Canada's repressive approach to "prostitution" is "being achieved in large measure *at the expense of the health and human rights of sex workers*" (emphasis added). Because the Canadian legislature de facto makes sex work illegal, it negatively affects the safety and health of female sex workers by forcing them to isolate themselves constantly so that they will not be arrested. This is also one of the conclusions of the Subcommittee on Solicitation Laws of the House of Commons (2006; emphasis added), which notes, "Criminalization intended to control prostitution-related activities in Canada *jeopardizes the safety of prostitutes*, as well as their access to health and social services."[6]

As researchers and various governmental reports on the subject have pointed out many times, the illegality of activities linked to sex work discourages female sex workers from pressing charges when they have been the victims of abuse or violence; they fear that they will be arrested or, at least, will not be taken seriously by police officers. A number of them mention that the current legislative context leads them to mistrust police officers, further isolate themselves, and practise their trade under conditions in which the risks of abuse increase, as to which the number of murders of sex workers unfortunately attests. Researchers John Lowman and Laura Fraser (1996) estimate that almost 80 percent of the women killed in British Columbia between 1975 and 1994 were street "prostitutes." Female sex workers who work on the street are 60 to 120 times more likely than are other workers to be severely assaulted or killed on the job (Lowman 2000; Lowman and Fraser 1996).[7]

This observation, though sad, is not new. Back in 1985, the Fraser Committee was aware of the difficult situation that female sex workers faced. Feeling that it was idealistic to envisage that "prostitution" would one day disappear, the committee suggested that "the criminal law relating to prostitution establishments should be drawn so as not to thwart the attempts of small numbers of prostitutes to organize their activities out of a place of residence" (Fraser Committee 1985, 538).

The ineffectiveness of the Canadian criminal statute and its negative effects on the safety of female sex workers was pointed out again in 1998 by the Federal/Provincial/Territorial Working Group on Prostitution (FPT Working Group). As it noted in its report (1998, 84), the amendments made to the *Criminal Code* over the previous twenty-five years had not led to the anticipated results, notably with regard to decreasing violence against "prostitutes." It also noted the existence of a link between violence against "prostitutes" and the place where the sex work takes place, the street generally being a more dangerous place than other sex-work contexts. The FPT Working Group (1998, 91) was also of the opinion that section 210 of the *Criminal Code* regarding bawdy-houses should be modified "to allow one or two prostitutes operating out of their own residence where municipalities believe that the hazards and dangers of street prostitution warranted such measures." Unfortunately, this recommendation, although made by both government reports, has remained a dead letter.

What is more, even today, section 210 harms female sex workers without really having an impact on the scope of "prostitution," contradicting claims by proponents of the repressive approach. The report of the Subcommittee on Solicitation Laws of the House of Commons (2006, Chapter Five) is clear on the subject: "According to some witnesses, prostitutes' family, social and working relationships are also disrupted by section 210, which states that anyone who visits the place where they sell their sexual services may be charged with being found in a common bawdy-house, no matter the reason for being there." This observation also is not new: in 1985, the Fraser Committee (1985, 593) had recommended that visiting or living in such a location not be an offence. Nora Currie and Kara Gillies (2006) also show that a number of female sex workers in abusive marital relationships are considered by social workers to be victims not of conjugal violence but of subjection to a pimp, even if this was not the case. It should also be noted that the justices in the *Bedford* case in the Court of Appeal for Ontario unanimously arrived at the same conclusion that this section of the *Criminal Code* threatens the safety of female sex workers and thus contravenes section 7 of the Canadian Charter of Rights and Freedoms. The justices opined,

> We conclude that the bawdy-house prohibition is overbroad because it captures conduct that is unlikely to lead to the problems Parliament seeks to curtail. In particular, the provisions prohibit a single prostitute operating discreetly by herself, in her own premises. We also agree with the application judge that the impact of the bawdy-house prohibition is grossly disproportionate to the legislative objective, because the record is clear that the safest way to sell sex is for a prostitute to work indoors, in a location under her control. It follows that the prohibition cannot be justified as a reasonable limit under s. 1.
>
> While we further agree with the application judge that the current bawdy-house prohibition is unconstitutional and must be struck down, we suspend the declaration of invalidity for 12 months to provide Parliament an opportunity to draft a Charter-compliant provision, should it elect to do so. (2012 ONCA 186, 74)

A similar observation was made concerning section 211 of the present *Criminal Code* – section 194 at the time – which forbade directing or transporting someone to a bawdy-house. In the view of the Fraser Committee (1985, 553), "In the first place [this provision] is so broad in its ambit that it embraces casual conduct which is by any standards unexceptional, for example, randomly directing a passerby to a bawdy house." In 2006, the Subcommittee on Solicitation Laws of the House of Commons noted that according to a number of witnesses, this inter-diction had the effect of "hinder[ing] the establishment of a safe, healthy environment in which persons may sell their sexual services" (Chapter Five). The same conclusion was reached for section 212 on procuring, which criminalizes the professional relations of female sex workers – that is, it may apply to co-renters, spouses, security guards, and all persons who live with or assist a female sex worker. The justices of the Court of Appeal for Ontario also concluded that application of this statute must be limited to "circumstances of exploitation" (2012 ONCA 186, 111).

Section 213 of the *Criminal Code*, on communication – by far the provision most frequently used by the police – is also used mainly against female sex workers, who are more often found guilty than are customers and, as a corollary, have longer criminal records. Data from the Canadian Centre for Justice Statistics for 2003-04 show, for example, that 68 percent of female sex workers prosecuted under section 213 of the *Criminal Code* are found guilty, compared to only 30 percent of customers. Worse, 92 percent of people sentenced to prison in connec-tion with adult "prostitution" are women (Subcommittee on Solicitation Laws 2006). As a number of researchers noted during hearings of the Subcommittee on Solicitation Laws in 2006, this criminalization "has made street prostitutes especially vulnerable to violence and abuse, as female sex workers are "more vulnerable to predation, robbery, harass-ment, and murder," and "they're unable to access help if they're in trouble."

Far from solving in any way the problem of "prostitution," the arrests of female sex workers under section 213, with the infractions and crim-inal records that ensue, force a number of them to find new customers in order to pay the resulting fines. What is more, those who want to change jobs are confronted with the handicap of a criminal record, which greatly inhibits their chances of success.

Conclusions of the Various Governmental Committees

Ironically (or sadly), repression, far from doing away with "prostitution," creates conditions that interfere with this objective by pushing the most vulnerable people to sell sexual services under ever-riskier conditions. This unfortunate observation has been made repeatedly by *all* official government reports, and yet nothing has been done to change a situation that is unbearable for female sex workers (Fraser Committee 1985; FPT Working Group 1998; Subcommittee on Solicitation Laws 2006). Table 1 shows the recurrence of certain observations by government committees with regard to criminalization of activities linked to "prostitution."

When "Prostitution" Is Seen as Slavery

The Neo-abolitionist Approach and Criminalization of Customers

Linked in certain ways to the repressive model that I have presented above, the neo-abolitionist approach aims to eradicate "prostitution" (Ekberg 2004; Louis 2000a, 2000b; Poulin 2004; Raymond 2004). Proponents of this legislative approach advocate repression of the purchase of sexual services – the customers – and not their sale, whether female sex workers are consenting or not. The laws in force in Sweden since 1999, and in Norway and Iceland since 2009, criminalize only customers and pimps, considered under all circumstances to be exploiters (Farley 2004; Raymond 2004).[8] In Sweden, for example, the purchase of casual sexual relations for payment, the promotion of casual sexual relations for remuneration, and conducting such activities are forbidden by law.

Female sex workers, however, can in no way be criminalized for the sale of sexual services. This paternalistic and infantilizing model systematically considers these workers to be victims who need help, whether there is violence or not, abuse or not. According to neo-abolitionists, no distinction should or can be made between "voluntary prostitution" and "forced prostitution" because even when individuals are deemed to

Table 1 Conclusions of the different governmental committees on the controversial use of criminal laws to control "prostitution"

	Section 210 (brothels)	Section 212 (procuring)	Section 213 (communication)	General comments on laws' effectiveness
Fraser Committee (1985)	Recommends partial decriminalization to allow female sex workers to work out of the home	Excessive scope of the law. Restrict its application to cases of use or threat of violence.	This is about not raising to an offence simply soliciting in the street but attacking public nuisances.	A need for legal and social reform, because the current rules are incoherent. Pointless to make the system more repressive, because it demeans and dehumanizes "prostitutes." Opportunities for exploitation must be eliminated by allowing private "prostitution."
FPT Working Group (1998)	Recommends that it be modified "to allow one or two prostitutes operating out of their own residence where municipalities believe that the hazards and dangers of street prostitution warranted such measures."		Did not have anticipated effects. Changed nothing with regard to safety of women. Used more against "prostitutes" than against customers.	The modifications of the past twenty-five years have been a failure, notably with regard to protection of "prostitutes." Link between violence against "prostitutes" and the place where the sex work is conducted: the street is generally more dangerous than other sites.
Subcommittee on Solicitation Laws of the House of Commons (2006)	Essentially is detrimental to female sex workers. Excessive scope of the law.	Excessive scope of the law. Criminalizes the professional relations of female sex workers.	Not effective in ensuring the safety of "prostitutes" and communities. Women are found guilty and sentenced more often are men.	"Criminalization intended to control prostitution-related activities in Canada *jeopardizes the safety of prostitutes*, as well as their access to health and social services." Contributes to increased secrecy of practice, which favours violence against women and puts them in an even weaker position.

be selling sexual services voluntarily, part of this decision is not really the result of their free will. This choice is presumed to be imposed on the individual by past or present living conditions that are beyond her control (see Chapter 1).

This sordid and one-dimensional image of female sex workers is restrictive and inadequate, and it impedes comprehension of the plurality of sex-work practices. There is no question of denying the existence of abusive situations – such situations arise in every trade. However, it seems essential to understand that many of these women take full responsibility for their reasoned and deliberate choice to sell sexual services for a myriad of personal reasons (extra income, being unemployed, for pleasure, for survival, and so on). In fact, the Subcommittee on Solicitation Laws of the House of Commons (2006, Chapter Two) notes "the variety of settings in which prostitution takes place and the resulting experiences."

Why Is Criminalization of Purchasing Sex Neither as Effective as Claimed nor Very Well Received by Female Sex Workers?[9]

Proponents of the Swedish model often emphasize its "effectiveness:" it is said to have reduced street "prostitution" by half by criminalizing customers. Looking more closely, the picture is not so black and white. First of all, we must consider the method used to assess a phenomenon that is, by its very nature, labile and "underground." In fact, both the Ministry of Justice (2004) and the National Board of Health and Welfare (2004) in Sweden have expressed doubts about the statistical data on the reduction of "prostitution." According to these authorities, it is difficult to assess accurately the situation in Sweden.[10] Similar to what occurred elsewhere when a repressive model was used with regard to sex work, the Swedish model led to changes to where and how sex work was practised rather than a reduction in the phenomenon. Customers and female sex workers apparently simply found new ways to organize their encounters after the law was adopted. Sweden's National Board of Health and Welfare noted that although "the number of persons selling sexual services seemed to have diminished in major urban centres after the law was introduced, numbers had not diminished on a national scale – the theory being prostitutes had left major urban centres and gone towards side streets in the suburbs."[11]

For example, female sex workers moved from downtown streets to more remote urban areas, worked in apartments and massage parlours, or used the Internet to meet new customers. As commissioner Per-Uno Hagestam, police chief of Stockholm, remarked in 2003 (quoted in *L'Express*, 3 April 2003), if street "prostitution" had disappeared – which was not the case – apartment "prostitution" had not disappeared, and had in fact slightly increased. Very likely, "prostitution" became less visible and more clandestine. This very secrecy puts female sex workers at greater risk of mistreatment and abuse. There is a correlation between the vulnerability of female sex workers and the fact that they are practising their trade in out-of-the-way places, where the risk of assault is higher (FPT Working Group 1998; Gemme 1993; Shaver 1996).

In short, far from having helped to reduce the purchase of sexual services, these laws simply changed the terms of practice and produced unanticipated effects that undermined women's safety. Since customers were now more likely to be apprehended by the police – who sometimes posed as female sex workers – customers are even more suspicious (see Chapter 3). The researchers of the European Network for HIV-STD Prevention in Prostitution (Europap/TAMPEP 4 1999) also noted the negative effects of criminalization of sex work on public health – for example, the lack of condoms, which could be used by police officers as evidence against customers to show that there had been "prostitution" activity.

Furthermore, in invariably considering the women who sell sexual services to be victims of their socioeconomic conditions (unemployment, violence, dysfunctional family, drug abuse, and so on), the neo-abolitionists seem to forget that exploitation and abuse are linked not to the nature of a particular job, such as sex work, but to the fact that this job is practised illegally or clandestinely. In all difficult or atypical trades, workers are likely to confront deplorable working conditions and abuse by customers or bosses. Yet prohibiting the professionalization of sex work will not make it possible to control abusers and swindlers and to improve female sex workers' working conditions, living conditions, and safety. Furthermore, a legal arsenal already exists in Canada and in many other Western countries to interdict and minimize these abusive situations. I shall return to this subject.

When the Sale of Sexual Services Is a Job To Be Controlled

The Regulationist Approach, or Legalization of "Prostitution"
Some countries, such as the Netherlands and Germany, as well as the state of Nevada in the United States, have opted for a regulationist approach, which uses a regulatory approach to sex work. The premise of this approach is that "prostitution" is here to stay and it is better to control its negative effects. For instance, based on the decision of the European Court of Justice, Germany deemed that the sale of sexual services is part of an economic strategy and that many individuals provide this service by choice and not because they are forced to.[12] The sale of sexual services is therefore permitted, and steps have been taken to improve civil and social protection of female sex workers (Brents and Hausbeck 2005; Brooks-Gordon 2006; Laskowski 2002).

Various legal measures have been created to regulate sex work, including the requirement that female sex workers and brothel operators hold permits. On the one hand, these individuals must pay income tax. Female sex workers are thus integrated, as Silke Ruth Laskowski (2002, 481) notes, "as equal participants in the important economic sector of the sex market." Standards for the physical layout of the workplace are also applied and regular inspections are conducted to ensure the quality and cleanliness of these establishments. On the other hand, street "prostitution" outside of designated zones is illegal, as it is in Nevada and the Netherlands (Brents and Hausbeck 2005; van Doorninck and Campbell 2006). In the Netherlands, the communes (municipalities) are responsible for issuing permits and setting conditions for running brothels within their borders. To obtain an operating permit, establishments must fulfil a number of obligations, such as respecting neighbourhood tranquillity, obeying city-planning regulations, and complying with certain hygiene standards (running water, use of condoms, minimum room dimensions, and so on). Municipal administrations are also responsible for ensuring that brothel operators respect these rules (van Doorninck and Campbell 2006, 69; see also Sénat français 2000, 31-34).

The regulationist approach therefore has several objectives. The first is to permit sex workers to benefit from complete social coverage (unemployment insurance, pension, and so on) when they work in designated premises. The second is to reduce health risks. Responsibility, integrity, and public safety are thus the values upon which The Hague has based its regulationist approach (Wagenaar 2006). Third, in parallel with the regulation of sex work (between consenting adults), the fight against "forced prostitution," "juvenile prostitution," and situations of abuse is maintained (Kilvington, Day, and Ward 2001; for Nevada, see Brents and Hausbeck 2005).

Why Does This Model Open the Door to Exploitation of Female Sex Workers?

The regulationist model, though interesting at first glance because it offers legal recognition of sex work under certain conditions, nevertheless poses numerous limitations on the full recognition of female sex workers. It starts with the principle that "prostitution" is a necessary evil and cannot be considered "real" work. This legislative model has been neither conceived nor formulated by the principals concerned – the female sex workers themselves. For example, in The Hague, female sex workers are not directly involved in the process of regulation (Wagenaar 2006). To put it another way, female sex workers have no real decision-making power in determining the working conditions imposed on them.

Somewhat like the situation that prevailed in the nineteenth century in some European countries (Corbin 1982), under the regulationist model the state appropriates the right and the duty to impose the rules that it deems necessary to reduce the harmful effects of sex work (for example, "public nuisances") without verifying the real needs of female sex workers, many of whom protest that brothel owners impose too many rules and that these rules do not adequately address their interests (Albert 2001; for Nevada, see Anderson 1995). Some female sex workers complain that it is illegal for them to work anywhere other than in the designated areas (van Doorninck and Campbell 2006) and claim that the priority is not to protect them but to collect taxes on their income (Farley 2004).[13] What is more, although the municipalities cannot unilaterally ban brothels within their borders, they have the power to complicate the operation of sex workers' establishments by instituting very strict rules (Wagenaar 2006).

It has also been noted that the existence of legal brothels – as in Nevada, for example – has encouraged the emergence of a double standard among female sex workers. On the one hand are those who work within legally authorized workplaces and agree to be subjected to rules imposed by a third party, whether these rules are suitable for them or not. On the other hand are those who do not (or cannot) follow these rules, including because they are too restrictive or unacceptable. These workers are de facto forced to work illegally. For instance, in Germany and the Netherlands, unlike in New Zealand – which has decriminalized sex work – many female sex workers cannot register officially with the authorities (Kilvington, Day, and Ward 2001).

Marieke van Doorninck and Rosie Campbell (2006, 72) note that since the new legislation was adopted in the Netherlands, migrant female sex workers, previously tolerated, are no longer able to work legally. In Germany, the European Network for HIV/STI Prevention and Health Promotion among Migrant Sex Workers (2007), financed by the European Commission, estimates that almost 60 percent of female sex workers are in this migratory situation. Thus, most of them find themselves without legal protection, made vulnerable by the forced secrecy of doing their work illegally, as they cannot obtain a work visa.[14] And, as van Doorninck and Campbell (2006, 73) rightly note, "if zones are so regulated that they are only open for licensed sex workers they will lose their original and important function of providing a safe place for sex workers. Marginalised groups will either choose not to go there or will not be permitted to work there."[15]

This is why I feel it is imperative to include female sex workers in the formulation of rules to govern their work. They are the best able to define how their trade should be supervised. Because the regulationist model ignores the expertise of female sex workers, the door is opened to abuse; this contrasts with the New Zealand law, which was developed in concert with female sex workers.[16]

For example, in Nevada, female sex workers working in the brothels are contractual workers, and this greatly limits their legal protection compared to that of employees (see Mensah 2002). Furthermore, it is up to the owner to determine the rules that female sex workers in her employ must follow. Since Nevada law favours the brothel owner, it is very difficult for female sex workers to negotiate their fair share of the receipts due to them from the sale of a sexual service (often, the owner takes 50 percent of the receipts[17]) or to negotiate fair working conditions (some owners require twelve to fourteen hours of work per day) (Mensah 2002). If alternative solutions are not found, female sex workers who refuse all owners' rules will be forced to work illegally.

When It Is Finally Time for Female Sex Workers to Decide

Why Should Sex Work Be Totally Decriminalized?

The statute in force in New Zealand since 2003 (and in New South Wales, Australia, since 1995) is built on the basic premise that in many situations the sale of sexual services is a personal choice and that female sex workers should be involved in regulating their working conditions – including the conditions of the workplace, the medical obligations, the fees, and so on.[18] In fact, this is the only legislative model in which female sex workers have been actively involved from the very beginning of the decriminalization process. This approach sets aside the moral positions presented above and prioritizes public health and human rights. The *Prostitution Reform Act* (2003) bill states,

> The purpose of this Act is to decriminalize prostitution (while not endorsing or morally sanctioning prostitution or its use) and to create a framework that –
>
> (a) safeguards the human rights of sex workers and protects them from exploitation;
> (b) promotes the welfare and occupational health and safety of sex workers;
> (c) is conducive to public health;
> (d) prohibits the use in prostitution of persons under 18 years of age;
> (e) implements certain other related reforms.

Thus, the New Zealand labour code applies to sex work as well as to other forms of atypical trades, but forms and practices involved in the purchase and sale of sexual services are the responsibility of the people involved in the sex industry and the law of the market. The sex industry is subjected to the same health and public safety regulations as are other industries in that country. In addition, the Ministry of Labour of New Zealand (via its Department of Occupational Safety and Health) has defined the guidelines for the various actors in the industry (workers, owners, employees, and so on) concerning their duties and responsibilities, notably with regard to safe sex, including information on the risk of sexually transmitted infections, use of a condom during sexual relations, and so on.[19]

In Canada, this approach (which would involve abrogation of sections 210, 211, 212, and 213 of the *Criminal Code*) is supported by a number of female sex workers' groups and by some community organizations and academics who feel that decriminalization of "prostitution" would better protect female sex workers against abuses related to the illegality of their work. Among the organizations is the Conseil permanent de la jeunesse du Québec, which recommended, in its report titled *Prostitution de rue: avis* (2004, 17), the decriminalization of "prostitution" in order to put an end to the growing violence and repression to which "prostitutes" are subjected. Opposing the approach of the neo-abolitionists, the authors of the report (2004, 17; our translation, emphasis added) were of the opinion that

> decriminalizing the activities of the prostitute while maintaining the criminalization of the customer *would not make* street prostitution practices safer. Indeed, in order to protect her income, the prostitute would have every interest in ensuring that customers are not incriminated, and, as a consequence, would encourage, once again, clandestine, often risky practices.

According to these authors, the current legislative situation engenders tensions among prostitutes, residents, community leaders, and the police, and these tensions are conducive to poor treatment and exploitation of female sex workers. The Canadian HIV/AIDS Legal Network also advocates full decriminalization of sex work in its report *Sex, Work,*

Rights: Reforming Canadian Criminal Laws on Prostitution (2005), as does the Canadian Medical Association, which, in the *Canadian Medical Association Journal* of 20 July 2004, exhorted physicians to pressure the federal government and politicians to "repeal all prostitution laws."[20]

Will Decriminalization Further Weaken Female Sex Workers?

According to some opponents, especially politicians,[21] decriminalizing sex work would be equivalent to leaving women to fend for themselves, with no legal recourse in the case of mistreatment by customers or pimps. Nothing could be less true. In New Zealand, sections 16 to 18 of the *Prostitution Reform Act* guarantee the safety of female sex workers.[22] Under section 16, anyone who tries to force a person to provide a sexual service against her will or to extract her income from the sexual services that she provides may be sentenced to fourteen years in prison. Section 17 authorizes female sex workers to refuse to provide a sexual service that they do not wish to perform, at any time during the exchange with the customer. Furthermore, a female sex worker may bring charges against a brothel manager who does not offer adequate working conditions.

In Canada, there are already a myriad of criminal laws that may (and should) be used to protect female sex workers when deplorable situations arise. If a customer or a "manager" (one who engages in procuring, according to the *Criminal Code*) refuses to pay or attempts to extort a female sex worker's money, section 346 of the *Criminal Code* in fact forbids extortion – that is, "Every one ... who, without reasonable justification or excuse and with intent to obtain anything, by threats, accusations, menaces or violence induces or attempts to induce any person, whether or not he is the person threatened, accused or menaced or to whom violence is shown, to do anything or cause anything to be done." If a customer or "manager" sexually or physically assaults a female sex worker, one may turn to sections 271 to 273 of the *Criminal Code* on sexual assault, or sections 265 to 269 on assault. According to section 265, "A person commits an assault when without the consent of another person, he applies force intentionally to that other person, directly or indirectly ... attempts or threatens, by an act or a gesture, to apply force to another person."

In New Zealand, female sex workers may bring charges against a customer who refuses to wear a condom, as safe sex is now a key feature in that country's legislation. After the *Prostitution Reform Act* was enacted, almost 90 percent of female sex workers who responded to a survey conducted by the Ministry of Justice of New Zealand (2005) stated that they felt they have legal protection, especially in terms of negotiating the use of a condom during sexual relations or refusing a recalcitrant customer. The people interviewed feel safer with regard to possible assaults, and, above all, they have the sense of being supported (Abel, Fitzgerald, and Brunton 2007).

The decriminalization of sex work in New Zealand has contributed greatly to raising awareness among the courts and police, which now take female sex workers' complaints seriously. The interviews conducted by Gillian Abel, Lisa Fitzgerald, and Cheryl Brunton (2007, 164ff) reveal that a number of female sex workers feel that their relations with the police improved after "prostitution" was decriminalized, particularly with regard to information about untoward events (customers refusing to pay, violence, insults, and so on). In addition, 60 percent of the participants in this study felt that police officers were now more concerned about their safety. Unlike what has happened in Sweden, decriminalization in New Zealand has encouraged social dialogue among female sex workers, communities, and police departments by forcing each group to respect the other as full citizens and workers. In Canada, it is obvious that the current criminal laws, which are supposed to protect female sex workers, essentially work against them and not against the customers.

And for those who fear that decriminalization would cause the number of female sex workers to mushroom, especially at street level, and thus create a greater public nuisance, Abel, Fitzgerald, and Brunton (2007) emphasize that decriminalization had no visible effects on the number of people entering the sex industries: the number of female sex workers remained stable between 1999 and 2007, and almost one-third of female sex workers worked independently – that is, without having to share the money they earned with a manager. Finally, contrary to what some claim, the refusal of an unemployed person to work in the sex industries can never affect the welfare payments to which he or she has the right.[23]

Will Decriminalization Reduce the Stigmatization of Female Sex Workers?

Some people lament that stigmatization of female sex workers in New Zealand did not really diminish with the decriminalization of their work. Of course, New Zealand's laws cannot be blamed for this lack of acceptance. Changing people's perceptions often takes a long time, and it is idealistic to believe that legislation or decriminalization of a behaviour will have an immediate impact on people's opinions. The example of homosexuality is probative in this regard. Although same-sex marriage was decriminalized thirty years ago – it is legal in a number of countries, including Canada – prejudice and homophobic violence persist (see Corriveau 2011). However, there is greater social acceptance of same-sex marriage, particularly among younger generations. There is no reason to believe that it would be otherwise for sex work, which would likely also gradually become socially acceptable.

Will Decriminalization Encourage Juvenile "Prostitution?"

Another spectre regularly raised by opponents to decriminalization concerns the supposed risk of an increase in juvenile "prostitution." Let's be clear: decriminalization of sex work neither interferes with nor represses "juvenile prostitution" or human trafficking, but it in no way impedes the repression of "juvenile prostitution," as demonstrated by the efforts used to eradicate these activities in all of the countries that have regulated (for example, the Netherlands and Germany) or decriminalized (for example, New Zealand) sex work. In these countries, even though sex work among consenting adults is authorized, criminal law strongly sanctions human trafficking, "forced prostitution," and "prostitution" involving children. "Adult prostitution" and "juvenile prostitution" are two distinct subjects, which may be treated independently of each other. In Canada, section 212 (2.1) of the *Criminal Code* specifically bans the procuring of persons under eighteen years of age. In other words, the decriminalization of practices surrounding the sale of sexual services among consenting adults would have no impact whatsoever on the illegality of juvenile prostitution.

Furthermore, Canada has ratified the United Nations' *Convention on the Rights of the Child*. It has committed itself to taking the measures necessary to impede and eliminate juvenile prostitution and to avoid children being encouraged to undertake illegal sexual activities. This will never change, whether or not Canada has the courage to legalize sex work among consenting adults.

A Needed Legislative Change: The Only Consensus on the Subject

For all the reasons that I have stated above, it is imperative to continue to pressure lawmakers to modify Canadian criminal law on "prostitution" as soon as possible – laws that have been criticized for more than thirty years in the government's own reports! The government has for too long hidden behind a false pretext, the lack of consensus, to justify its inaction.

It is delusional to believe that there will be social consensus on a subject as sensitive as the sale of sexual services. Recent history, however, has thrown the relevance of consensus as a criterion into doubt: abolition of the death penalty, same-sex marriage, and the right to abortion all became law even though a significant number of Canadians opposed the new legislation. We must therefore conclude that what our politicians lack is the political courage to protect and adequately respect female sex workers. In any event, when we think about it, three consensuses already exist: first, on the need to better protect female sex workers; second, on the failure of the laws in force to do away with "prostitution"; and third, on the fact that the current laws essentially harm female sex workers.

Although there is no unanimity – neither among feminist groups nor among groups of female sex workers and researchers – on what should be done to improve the situation, all agree that the current legal situation is *untenable* because it makes female sex workers more vulnerable to assault and abuse of all types due to the illegality of their work. The 171 murders of female sex workers listed in Canada between 1991 and 2004 (Statistics Canada 2006) should convince us of this. It is *this* consensus that should serve as the basis for decision makers to change an unsustainable and dangerous situation that goes counter to the principles of equality among citizens who defend the Canadian Charter of Rights and Freedoms, as the justices of the Court of Appeal for Ontario remind us in the *Bedford* ruling of March 2012. Finally, we must listen to the principals concerned – female sex workers – when we decide what modifications to make.

Notes

1 In 1983, the *Criminal Code of Canada* was finally modified so that the word "prostitute" applied to people of both sexes. S.C. 1980-83, c. 125, art. 11.
2 See *R. v Hutt* (1978) 2 S.C.C. 476; *R. v Whitter* and *R. v Galjot* (1981) 2 S.C.C. 606. In *R. v Hutt* (1978), for example, the Supreme Court of Canada ruled that there was solicitation only when it could be established that there was proof the accused had acted in a *pressing or persistent* manner. In *R. v Whitter* and *R. v Galjot* (1981), the Supreme Court of Canada ruled that the pressing or persistent behaviour had to be *directed toward one customer in particular* and could not consist of a series of advances to potential customers.
3 Some see this approach to sex work not as repressive but as tolerant. In my view, however, the Canadian approach is far from tolerant, as the current statute criminalizes different facets of sex work, making it impossible for workers to work legally. The many and repeated police raids on female sex workers in Canadian cities also indicate that the Canadian model is more repressive than tolerant.
4 A female sex worker may legally respond directly to a call from a "real" customer.
5 *R. v Richer* (1994), 64 Q.A.C. 71, [1994] J.Q. n. 472 (C.A.) (our translation).
6 See Subcommittee on Solicitation Laws of the House of Commons, Chapter Five (2006), http://www.parl.gc.ca/HousePublications/Publication.aspx?DocId=2599932&Language=E&Mode=1&Parl=39&Ses=1&File=192.
7 According to Potterat et al. (2004), female sex workers are seventeen times more likely to be murdered than is the general female population in a corresponding age group.
8 For instance, Raymond (2004, 1158) observes, "Instead of abandoning women in the sex industry to state sponsored prostitution, the Swedish Law addresses the predatory actions of men who buy women for the sex of prostitution. Recognizing the inseparability of prostitution and trafficking, the Law states, 'Prostitution and trafficking in women are seen as harmful practices that cannot, and should not be separated;' in order to effectively eliminate trafficking in women, concrete measures against prostitution must be put in place."
9 For revealing testimonials on the harmful effects of the Swedish model, see the excellent site http://www.cybersolidaires.org/. See also the article of 3 October 2005, "Être travailleuse du sexe en Suède: un enfer rempli de dangers."
10 See www.regjeringen.no/nb/dep/jd/dok/rapporter_planer/rapporter/2004/Purchasing-Sexual-Services.html?id=106214; http://www.childcentre.info/projects/exploitation/sweden/dbaFile11751.pdf; www.childcentre.info/projects/exploitation/

sweden/dbafile11751.pdf. For an excellent methodological critique on attempts to assess the scope of prostitution, see Mathieu (2009).

11 Quoted in Chapter Six of the Subcommittee on Solicitation Laws (2006). See also http://tampep.eu; Kilvington, Day, and Ward (2001).

12 According to the European Court of Justice, prostitution is "a provision of services for remuneration which ... falls within the concept of economic activities." See article 2, ECJ, C-268/99, ECR, 2001, I-8615, par. 33, 49, quoted in Laskowski (2002, 479).

13 With regard to zones reserved for sex work, for example, van Doorninck and Campbell (2006, 70) note, "A general complaint from sex workers about these designated zones is that they are too small[,] which heightens competition between sex workers (Ten Dan et al., 1999). These zones are also far away from city centres and it is either expensive (taxi) or dangerous (walking through a desolated area) to get to the zone." The Home Office (2004) observes that the Netherlands model is considered a failure, since a number of female sex workers offer their services outside of the designated zone.

14 See Europap/TAMPEP 4 (1999).

15 On this subject, van Doorninck and Campbell (2006) note that the zones reserved for sex work that are the safest and the most "functional," from the point of view of both the female sex workers and the authorities, are those that are less regulated – that is, those that best adapt to social changes.

16 See Healy (2006).

17 According to the European Network for HIV/STI Prevention and Health Promotion among Migrant Sex Workers (TAMPEP) (2007), German and foreign female sex workers keep about 50 percent of their gross income when they work for a third party. See http://tampep.eu.

18 For more information, see Ministry of Justice of New Zealand (2005), www. legislation.govt.nz/act/public/2003/0028/latest/DLM197815.html.

19 As Abel, Fitzgerald, and Brunton (2007, 23-24) note, the Prostitution Law Reform Committee stated that the guidelines "also outlined requirements for sex worker health, workplace amenities and psychosocial factors, such as security and safety from violence, alcohol, drugs, smoking in the workplace, complaints, employee participation and workplace documents."

20 http://www.cmaj.ca/content/171/2/109.full.pdf+html.

21 See the debates of the Subcommittee on Solicitation Laws held during the first session of the 38th Parliament.

22 For more details, consult the *Prostitution Reform Act* (2003), www.legislation.govt. nz/act/public/2003/0028/latest/DLM197815.html.

23 "Refusal to work as a sex worker also does not affect any entitlements to a benefit under the Social Security Act 1964 or the Injury, Prevention, Rehabilitation, and Compensation Act 2001" (Abel, Fitzgerald, and Brunton 2007, 25).

References

Abel, Gillian, Lisa Fitzgerald, and Cheryl Brunton. 2007. *The Impact of the Prostitution Reform Act on the Health and Safety Practices of Sex Workers.* Christchurch: New Zealand Prostitution Law Review Committee.

Albert, Alexa. 2001. *Brothel: Mustang Ranch and Its Women.* New York: Random House.

Anderson, Laura. 1995. *Working in Nevada.* www.bayswan.org/Laura.html.

Brents, Barbara G., and Kathryn Hausbeck. 2005. Violence and Legalized Brothel Prostitution in Nevada: Examining Safety, Risk, and Prostitution Policy. *Journal of Interpersonal Violence* 20 (3): 270-95.

Brooks-Gordon, Belinda. 2006. *The Price of Sex: Prostitution, Policy, and Society.* Portland: Willan Publishing.

Canadian HIV/AIDS Legal Network. 2005. *Sex, Work, Rights: Reforming Canadian Criminal Laws on Prostitution.* Toronto: Canadian HIV/AIDS Legal Network.

Canadian Medical Association. 2004. Prostitution Laws: Health Risks and Hypocrisy [editorial]. http://www.cmaj.ca/content/171/2/109.full.pdf+html.

Conseil permanent de la jeunesse du Québec. 2004. *Prostitution de rue: avis.* Quebec City: Gouvernement du Québec.

Corbin, Alain. 1982. *Les filles de noces. Misère sexuelle et prostitution au xixe siècle.* Paris: Flammarion, "Champs" imprint.

Corriveau, Patrice. 2011. *Judging Homosexuals: A History of Gay Persecution in Quebec and France,* trans. Käthe Roth. Vancouver: UBC Press.

Currie, Nora, and Kara Gillies. 2006. *Bound by the Law: How Canada's Protectionist Policies in the Areas of Both Rape and Prostitution Limit Women's Choices, Agency and Activities.* Unpublished manuscript. Funded by Status of Women.

Ekberg, Gunilla. 2004. The Swedish Law that Prohibits the Purchase of Sexual Services: Best Practices for Prevention of Prostitution and Trafficking in Human Beings. *Violence Against Women* 10 (10): 1187-1218.

Europap/TAMPEP 4. 1999. *Policies on Sex Work and Health.* London: Europap/TAMPEP 4. tampep.eu/.

European Network for HIV/STI Prevention and Health Promotion among Migrant Sex Workers (TAMPEP). 2007. *National Report on HIV and Sex Work. Germany.* Amsterdam: TAMPEP international Foundation.

Farley, Melissa. 2004. "Bad for the Body, Bad for the Heart": Prostitution Harms Women Even If Legalized or Decriminalized. *Violence Against Women* 10 (10): 1087-1125.

Federal/Provincial/Territorial Working Group on Prostitution. 1998. *Report and Recommendations in Respect of Legislation, Policy and Practices Concerning Prostitution-Related Activities.* Ottawa: Department of Justice Canada.

Fraser Committee (Special Committee on Pornography and Prostitution). 1985. *Pornography and Prostitution in Canada: Report of the Special Committee on Pornography and Prostitution.* Ottawa: Government of Canada, Department of Justice, Supply and Services.

Gemme, Robert. 1993. Évaluation de la répression de la prostitution de rue à Montréal de 1970 à 1991. *Revue Sexologique* 1 (2): 161-92.

Healy, Catherine. 2006. Decriminalizing Our Lives and Our Work: The New Zealand Model. In *eXXXpressions: Forum XXX Proceedings*, ed. Émilie Cantin, Jenn Clamen, Jocelyne Lamoureux, Maria Nengeh Mensah, Pascale Robitaille, Claire Thiboutot, Louise Toupin, and Francine Tremblay, 96-99. Montreal: Stella. cybersolidaires. typepad.com/ameriques/2006/06/par_catherine_h.html.

Home Office. 2004. *Paying the Price: A Consultation Paper on Prostitution*. London: Home Office.

Kilvington, Judith, Sophie Day, and Helen Ward. 2001. European Prostitution Policy: A Time of Change? *Feminist Review* 67: 78-93.

Laskowski, Silke Ruth. 2002. The New German Prostitution Act: An Important Step to a More Rational View of Prostitution as an Ordinary Profession in Accordance with European Community Law. *International Journal of Comparative Labour Law and Industrial Relations* 18 (4): 479-91.

Louis, Marie-Victoire. 2000a. Pour construire l'abolitionnisme du xxie siècle. Interview, *Cahiers marxistes* 216: 123-51.

–. 2000b. Vers la marchandisation légale du corps humain? Non à l'Europe proxénète. *Femmes info* 89.

Lowman, John. 2000. Violence and the Outlaw Status of (Street) Prostitution in Canada. *Violence Against Women* 6 (9): 987-1011.

Lowman, John, and Laura Fraser. 1996. Violence against Persons Who Prostitute: The Experience in British Columbia. *Technical Report No. TR1996-14*. Ottawa: Department of Justice Canada.

Mathieu, Lilian. 2009. Ce que le mélange entre expertise et militantisme peut produire de pire ... *Contretemps*, contretemps.eu/socio-flashs/ce-que-melange -entre-expertise-militantisme-peut-produire-pire.

Mensah, Maria Nengeh. 2002. Réponse au comité du Bloc Québécois sur la prostitution de rue. Montreal: Stella, l'amie de Maimie, www.chezstella.org/stella/ ?q=node/107.

Ministry of Justice of New Zealand. 2003. *Prostitution Reform Act 2003*, http://www. legislation.govt.nz/act/public/2003/0028/latest/DLM197815.html.

–. 2005. *The Nature and Extent of the Sex Industry in New Zealand: An Estimation*. http://www.justice.govt.nz/publications/global-publications/t/the-nature-and -extent-of-the-sex-industry-in-new-zealand-an-estimation.

Ministry of Justice, Sweden. 2004. *Purchasing Sexual Services in Sweden and the Netherlands*. www.regjeringen.no/nb/dep/jd/dok/rapporter_planer/rapporter/ 2004/Purchasing-Sexual-Services.html?id=106214.

National Board of Health and Welfare [Sweden]. 2004. Prostitution in Sweden 2003 – Knowledge, Beliefs and Attitudes of Key Informants. http://www.socialstyrelsen. se/Lists/Artikelkatalog/Attachments/10488/2004-131-28_200413128.pdf.

Potterat, John J., Devon D. Brewer, Stephen Q. Muth, Richard B. Rothenberg, Donald E. Woodhouse, John B. Muth, Heather K. Sites, and Stuart Brody. 2004. Mortality in a Long-term Open Cohort of Prostitute Women. *American Journal of Epidemiology* 159: 778-85.

Poulin, Richard. 2004. *La mondialisation des industries du sexe. Prostitution, pornographie, traite des femmes et des enfants.* Ottawa: L'interligne.

Raymond, Janice G. 2004. Prostitution on Demand: Legalizing the Buyers as Sexual Consumers. *Violence Against Women* 10 (10) 1156-86.

Sénat français. 2000. *Le Régime juridique de la prostitution féminine.* France: Sénat.

Shaver, Frances. 1996. Occupational Health and Safety on the Dark Side of the Service Industry. In *Post-Critical Criminology,* ed. Thomas O'Reilly-Fleming, 42-55. Scarborough: Prentice-Hall Canada.

Statistics Canada. 2006. *Measuring Violence Against Women: Statistical Trend.* Ottawa: Statistics Canada.

Subcommittee on Solicitation Laws of the House of Commons. 2006. *The Challenge of Change: A Study of Canada's Criminal Prostitution Laws.* Ottawa: House of Commons.

United Nations. 1995. *Report of the Fourth World Conference on Women,* Beijing, 4-15 September, A/Conf.177/20.

Van Doorninck, Marieke, and Rosie Campbell. 2006. "Zoning" Street Sex Work: The Way Forward. In *Sex Work Now,* ed. Rosie Campbell and Maggie O'Neil, 62-91. Portland: Willan Publishing.

Wagenaar, Hendrik. 2006. Democracy and Prostitution: Deliberating the Legalization of Brothels in the Netherlands. *Administration and Society* 38 (2): 198-235.

The *Work* of Sex Work

3

CHRIS BRUCKERT AND COLETTE PARENT

Prostitution has long been referred to as the world's oldest profession. It is striking, therefore, that the women and men labouring in this profession have rarely been defined as workers in either popular discourse or academic analysis. It was not until sex workers started to organize, redraw the boundaries of the debate, speak about their work, and defend their interests in groups such as CORP, COYOTE, the PROS Network, and Maggie's that the term "sex work" was widely adopted. The phrase represents much more than a linguistic subtlety. It reflects a powerful political intervention that undermines normative assumptions and compels reconsideration not only of the sex industry and those that labour within it but of the relegation of sexuality to the private realm.

In this chapter, we explore street-based, out-call, and in-call sex work as particular types of work by drawing on a framework that straddles labour theory, sociology of work, and criminology. Such a lens is a fruitful point of entry. Most importantly, thinking about sex work as work is consistent with the subjective position of those who labour in the sex industry. Moreover, this theoretical point of entry allows us to outline parallels with other jobs; situate the industry within broader labour market trends; shed light on often invisible labour structures, processes, skills, and challenges; and draw attention to diversity by highlighting the differences within and between industry sectors. At the same time, of course, sex work is not work like any other: it is stigmatized and marginalized and criminalized.[1] It is for these reasons that we must integrate insights from criminology in order to reflect on the ways that socio-legal discourses and practices condition the labour of workers, increase the risks they confront, exacerbate their stress and marginalization, and shape the relations of workers to their social and personal worlds.

As we explained in Chapter 1, it is imperative that our understanding be based not on morality, conjecture, or manipulated statistics but on solid empirical research. In this chapter, we draw on studies that we have conducted with street-based, in-call, and out-call workers[2] and on the growing body of literature that has emerged in Canada over the course of the past twenty years (see Benoit and Millar 2001; Bruckert and Chabot 2010; Jeffrey and MacDonald 2006; Law 2011; Lewis and Shaver 2006; Lowman 2000; Lowman and Fraser 1996; O'Doherty 2011; Pivot 2004, 2006; Van der Meulen, Durisin, and Love 2013). This solid empirical research, grounded in the experiences of workers, eschews moralistic assumptions in favour of rigorous studies designed to tease out complexity and draw attention to issues of violence, marginality, and stigma.

How Is the Sex Industry Structured?

Labour theory enables us to step outside of the traditional criminological analysis of deviance in order to examine these jobs as *jobs*. We start by considering how the labour is organized. The dominant image of sex work is a woman soliciting for customers in a public space. In fact, although the majority of *Criminal Code* charges for prostitution-related offences are laid against street-based sex workers and their customers,[3] this sector represents just a small part of the industry.[4] Most sex workers labour in the out-call (providing services in the homes or hotel rooms of clients) and in-call (providing services to clients who come to their place of business) sectors. Within each sector, there is a considerable range in terms of services provided, rate scales, and payment structure. For example, street-based workers usually work within a fee-for-service structure, whereas those in the in-call and out-call sectors may work as escorts and be paid by the hour, or they may be compensated in a fee-for-service structure, or a combination of the two. Whether the worker is independent or works with or for a third party is a particularly significant factor.

Independent sex workers – including, according to many research-ers, the overwhelming majority of street-based sex workers (see, for example, Benoit and Millar 2001; Bruckert and Chabot 2010; Jeffrey and MacDonald 2006; Pivot 2004) – establish for themselves when and where they will work and what services they will provide. Moreover, within market constraints, they also determine the fees they will charge.[5] By contrast, the labour structure of sex workers who work for or with third parties (in, for example, escort agencies, dungeons, brothels, and massage parlours) is comparable to that of many other service-sector workers in the new economy. Like aestheticians, massage therapists, and hairstylists, for example, these workers are "disguised" employees. On the one hand, they are denied the income security, access to statutory protection, and legal recourse generally associated with employment. On the other hand, they are managed like employees. They are scheduled for shifts during which they must be on-site or available;[6] labour prac-tices are stipulated, sometimes including what services are to be offered; they are subject to labour-site expectations (for instance, management may specify attire); and there is sometimes an expectation of "free" labour (such as receptionist duties and cleaning). Moreover, in these cases, fee scales are determined by management; in our research on sex work in erotic establishments in Montreal and Toronto, workers received, in general, between 40 and 60 percent of the fees (see Bruckert and Law 2013; Bruckert, Parent, and Robitaille 2003; Parent and Bruckert 2005).[7]

The relationship with management is variable. Although some man-agers and owners of erotic establishments and escort agencies (who are vulnerable to charges under sections 210 and 212 of the *Criminal Code,* respectively) economically and/or sexually exploit their employ-ees, others offer workers a number of useful and valuable business services, such as administration, physical space, equipment, secretarial services, and advertising (see, for example, Bruckert and Law 2013; Bruckert, Parent, and Robitaille 2003; Currie and Gillies 2006; Lowman 2000; Parent and Bruckert 2005). They also offer security measures such as drivers and client screening. In in-call establishments, there may also be alarms, security cameras at the entrances, a (real or virtual) bouncer, the eviction of violent customers, and regulated access.[8]

In stark contrast to the image put forward in the popular press,[9] it is evident that workers balance the relative advantages and disadvantages of each labour structure (as they see them at the time) and may elect to change sectors in response to shifting personal, social, or economic realities. For example, street-based sex workers are at greatest risk of arrest (under section 213 of the *Criminal Code*), violence, and stigmatization; however, the labour structure affords them a great deal of flexibility and autonomy, which allows them to adjust their labour schedule to meet their particular circumstances (children and other responsibilities). It also permits them to retain all of their earnings. Similarly, in-call and out-call workers may choose to work as independents to ensure that they retain control over their labour conditions, hours, and earnings (and also sometimes to avoid working collectively) (see Bruckert, Parent, and Robitaille 2003; Jeffrey and MacDonald 2006, 29-35; Parent and Bruckert 2005). Some workers, however, do not want, or do not feel able, to be entrepreneurs; they may lack the interest or the skills, or they may perceive the sex industry to be a temporary, short-term measure. For such individuals, investing in attracting clients and building up a business (which could entail having pictures taken, setting up a Web site, advertising, developing a client list, and receiving reviews on client review sites) is not in their interest (Bruckert, Parent, and Robitaille 2003; Parent and Bruckert 2005. See also Stella 2009).

The decision whether to work in the in-call or out-call sector may also be influenced by a worker's reflections on risk. In in-call establishments, workers have a measure of security: they are assured that help is available if they are physically or sexually assaulted or robbed; clients are presumably less likely to assault a worker in the vicinity of potential witnesses; and aggressors may be deterred by the potential for arrest (see Benoit and Millar 2001; Jeffrey and MacDonald 2006). In spite of the security afforded by in-call establishments, some workers elect to work in the out-call sector in order to avoid the potential of being charged under section 210 of the *Criminal Code*. Such workers make a conscious decision to forgo the greater security of the in-call site in an attempt to minimize their risk of criminalization (Bruckert and Chabot 2010).

Labour Process and Practices

The labour lens also allows us to shift from structure to practices – or what workers *do* (Phillips 1997) – positions us to consider the nature of the labour, and renders skills and competencies visible. Underlining the importance of not conflating labour market sectors, in this section we shed light on diversity as we examine how labour practices are conditioned by the criminalized context.

Skills and Competencies

Like much consumer-service–sector employment, sex work is physically demanding labour that requires stamina and physical strength. In stark contrast to the discourse that suggests that sex work is somehow natural and therefore not really *work* (and certainly not *skilled* work), success is contingent on the development of a particular and not uncomplicated skill set (see Jeffrey and MacDonald 2006; Law 2011; Parent and Bruckert 2005). As is the case in many other jobs in the service sector, interpersonal skills are essential. Like waitresses, hair stylists, and sales clerks, sex workers have to be sociable, patient, courteous, polite, and capable of dealing with a variety of people. They must present a pleasant and professional demeanour to customers. They also have to be able to rapidly gauge a customer, identify the customer's needs, and put the customer at ease. As Tuulia Law (2011) argues, many of these skills, including money management, communication and listening, conflict resolution, marketing and business administration, time management, assertiveness, and creativity, are transferable to jobs outside the sex industry.

There are also a number of more specialized prerequisites for success, including an open attitude toward sexuality. Depending on the services they provide, workers must have basic anatomic and sexual knowledge, be able to create and maintain an erotic and pleasing presentation of themselves, and discern and respond to customers' (often non-verbalized) needs or wishes. The application of these skills in the context of the commercial encounter is complex: the worker must be able to control the interaction, be vigilant with respect to any danger of assault, set boundaries, and assert authority as a professional while simultaneously creating a sensual environment, establishing a pleasant relationship with the customer, and, in some cases, carrying out a sexual fantasy. This last expectation also speaks to acting skills. Of course, sexual techniques are also a requirement, although again, contrary to the dominant discourses, sex workers are discerning about what services they are prepared to offer, to whom, and under what circumstances. For example, street-based and in-call workers may offer oral and/or manual release only, whereas domination workers may refuse to offer either of these services (Parent and Bruckert 2005, 2006).[10]

In addition, there are specific skills that are conditioned by sector and the particular labour arrangement: in-call workers employed in massage parlours require knowledge of the human body and massage techniques. Escorts, whether in- or out-call, are paid by the hour and are frequently called upon to offer intimacy and social interaction, in addition to, and sometimes in lieu of, sexual services. In domination and submission, workers are required to be not only competent with the apparatus but also able to respond to customers' requests while at the same time gauging their specific reactions to the stimulus used (Bruckert, Parent, and Robitaille 2003; Parent and Bruckert 2005). Independent workers, regardless of sector, must also draw upon entrepreneurial skills as they administer their small business, including establishing and maintaining a regular client base and promoting and selling their services.

Why Work as a Sex Worker?

As we have seen, workers in the sex industry face many challenges. This, of course, begs the question *why* someone would decide to work as a sex worker. Thinking about sex work as work allows us to transcend neo-liberal rhetoric about choice and to appreciate that sex workers, *like any other workers,* are selecting their labour location within the context of a *constrained* range of options. In Canada, not only do working-class women continue to be ghettoized in sales, service, and clerical occupations (Statistics Canada 2005b), but the post-industrial labour market is increasingly characterized by "McJobs" (Ritzer 2004, 148): low-paid, deskilled, monotonous, and highly monitored service sector work that offers workers neither satisfaction nor stability – nor, for that matter, a living wage (Ritzer 2004, 108-15). In this context, sex work offers workers the opportunity to make an income that will meet their needs as well as afford them the independence, status, and sense of self-worth associated with financial security (Penney 1983, 21). It is not just a question of money and whether or not a job meets middle-class and moralistic standards of desirability; there are clearly secondary (non-economic) benefits derived from participation in this labour sector. Sex workers appreciate the autonomy, the chance to meet and interact with new and interesting people, the opportunity to explore their sexuality, and the sense of accomplishment related to doing a job well. Finally, as it does for other job sites, the work can (for street-based workers or those who labour in an establishment) provide social contacts, camaraderie, and friendships.

The Spectre of the Law

All workers' labour practices are conditioned by the particular context in which the labour occurs. In the case of sex workers, this context includes the potential for arrest and criminalization,[11] which would jeopardize their employment and income (if the establishment or agency were to be closed, or if charges were to be laid against them or their employers), their freedom and time (if they were to be convicted of a criminal offence), and their future mobility and prospects for careers and employment outside of the sex industry (if they were to be convicted of a criminal offence). In general, in an effort to decrease the likelihood of being criminally charged, sex workers monitor their use of language. For example, they avoid reference to the provision of sexual services when they communicate with potential customers, preferring instead to use euphemistic phrases such as "happy endings" and "California massage." The use of coded language to avoid being criminally charged can result in misunderstandings regarding, for example, services and fees. Potential customers (who do not necessarily understand the code) may decline, or they may respond aggressively when they do not receive the anticipated services or when the cost is higher than anticipated (Bruckert, Parent, and Robitaille 2003; Parent and Bruckert 2005).

Street-based sex workers also take other measures: in order to avoid being readily identified as sex workers and drawing attention to themselves, they adjust their self-presentation by, for example, not wearing attire traditionally associated with sex work, such as high heels and short skirts, and opting for a less conspicuous appearance. They also adapt their labour practices (by working alone, by working in isolated areas, by not taking the time to properly assess clients). These tactics can have negative implications, including making it more challenging to attract customers, increasing the time required to earn their money, and, as we will see below, rendering them more vulnerable to violence.

How Is Sex Work *Not* Like Other Work?

As noted in the introduction, sex work is work, but it is stigmatized, criminalized, and marginalized work. We now bring these differences into sharper focus by attending to questions of violence and health as well as (the lack of) labour and police protection. We conclude the chapter with an examination of issues of stigmatization in order to draw attention to the implications of moral judgment, legal discourses, and criminal justice practices on the private lives of workers in the sex industry.

Violence

The extraordinary high levels of violence, including fatal violence, perpetrated against sex workers is well documented in academic and legal literature (see, for example, Benoit and Millar 2001; Bruckert and Chabot 2010; Cler-Cunningham and Christensen 2001; Jeffrey and MacDonald 2006; Lewis and Shaver 2006; Lowman 2000; Lowman and Fraser 1996) and was recognized by the Parliamentary Subcommittee on Solicitation Laws (2006). A 2006 Statistics Canada report stated that 171 female sex workers were murdered between 1991 and 2004, and 45 percent of these murders remained unsolved (the authors noted that "violence against sex workers often goes unnoticed" [2006a, 39]).[12] As the lower rates of violence against sex workers in countries such as New Zealand attest (Abel, Fitzgerald, and Brunton 2008), such violence is not inherent to the labour but is, at least in part, a result of the particular social, legal, and labour context in which it is situated. Not surprisingly, workers' susceptibility to violence and their strategies for managing the risk of robbery, physical aggression, and sexual assault are influenced by the labour process and therefore differ by labour sector.

Street-based sex workers are the most vulnerable not only to criminalization but also to violence from diverse sources, including the police, community members, customers, and aggressors (Bruckert and Chabot 2010; Jeffrey and MacDonald 2006). Workers speak of physical violence perpetrated by the police; incidents reported range from being beaten, kicked, and pepper-sprayed to being aggressively handled during arrest and subjected to strip-searches by men.[13] They also experience verbal abuse, including being publicly belittled, being called names, and being stopped even when they are obviously not working. These workers, highly cognizant of power relations, feel powerless to reduce their vulnerability to these assaults except by avoiding contact with the police. Similarly, workers perceive themselves to have limited options when confronted with verbal assaults (such as insults and name calling) and physical assaults (such as objects being thrown at them) by individual members of the community or when they are targeted in organized anti–sex-work campaigns that single out their homes and repeatedly harass them.[14]

Sex workers are also vulnerable to violence perpetrated by aggressors and sometimes by clients as well. The distinction between the two is important. The former is an individual who may present himself as a customer but whose intention is to inflict physical, sexual, or financial harm. Lowman (2000) refers to these actions as predatory violence and notes that they are premeditated; by contrast, a client is an individual who seeks out and pays for the agreed-upon sexual services from a sex worker. Violence perpetuated by this population is situational violence that generally arises out of a dispute over fees or services.[15] To protect themselves from violence by disgruntled clients and aggressors, street-based sex workers employ a range of tactics, including trusting their intuition; sharing information with other workers; having clients park in a space known to them; relying on regular clients; being assertive with clients; providing good service and being ethical in interactions; being alert (for instance, avoiding the use of substances while working); and remaining calm during the assault in order to minimize injury. Others, cognizant that they could be charged for a weapons offence, nonetheless arm themselves (for instance, with a knife or pepper spray), arguing that they have little choice but to take responsibility for their own safety.

Unfortunately, their efforts notwithstanding, street-based sex workers are made more vulnerable to violence when they employ strategies to avoid the attention of the police (and thereby reduce the likelihood that they will be criminally charged or harassed). The implications of this are serious; Lowman (2000) has shown that there is a correlation between the introduction of *Criminal Code* section 213 and increased levels of violence, including fatal violence, against sex workers. The nature of the relationship between avoidance of the police and violence is multi-faceted. First, when workers seek to evade the attention of the police, they will shift their solicitation to less-populated or less-residential areas and avoid conspicuous locations (such as storefronts). Should a worker be attacked in a less-populated area, there is a reduced chance that assistance will be readily available. Moreover, there are fewer witnesses. This means that aggressors may target street-based sex workers, knowing that there is limited risk of their being arrested (Lowman 2000).

Second, one of the traditional tactics that sex workers have employed is to work with a colleague and write down (or appear to write down) the licence plate number of each other's customers' cars (see Bruckert, Parent, and Pouliot 2006; Jeffrey and MacDonald 2006; Lewis and Shaver 2006). Using the same logic as for any other type of surveillance initiative (such as that used by stores when they install video surveillance equipment), the workers presume that their actions will deter potential aggressors. This approach is abandoned when workers fear drawing the attention of the police because they are working in pairs (Bruckert, Parent, and Pouliot 2006). Third, workers in this sector report that they rely on instinct to determine if a potential client poses a security risk – instinct that is based on their experiential knowledge and ability to read multiple small indicators. The efficacy of this strategy is contingent on the worker taking adequate time to assess the potential client – something that workers are less likely to do when they are seeking to avoid police attention. Moreover, during intense police activity, all customers (who are also vulnerable to charges under *Criminal Code* section 213) are likely to appear nervous, making it difficult for workers to accurately assess the risk posed by an individual (Norwegian Working Group 2004).

Street-based sex workers are also rendered more vulnerable to violence when police target customers in "anti-john campaigns," some of which, such as the Ottawa Police Services' current "community safety letters," use extra-legal tactics. Such police activity may reduce the customer base, which will, in turn, increase competition among workers and the likelihood of their taking chances with questionable customers or offering services (such as oral sex without a condom) that they would not be prepared to offer under customary market conditions or decreasing their fees. The last tactic means that workers will have to provide services to more customers to make adequate money; this, in turn, increases their risk of both assault and arrest.

In-call and out-call workers are, by virtue of their labour structure, much less vulnerable to violence by community members and police;[16] however, they, too, risk physical and sexual assaults. In particular, out-call workers, who provide services in customers' homes or hotel rooms, are highly cognizant of their vulnerability and, like street-based workers, take measures to protect themselves from the risk of physical and sexual assault. Those who work through an agency can draw on resources such as the driver and client screening/verification. There is also an element of deterrence, as customers are aware that the worker's whereabouts are known and recorded by agency personnel. Independent workers also take measures, such as always informing a friend of their destination (leaving the information in a note or sending a text message upon arrival, sometimes ensuring that the client sees them doing so), confirming the address via the Internet, never consuming illicit substances with customers and being very prudent in the consumption of alcohol, not providing submission services, meeting new customers in public places, and providing services in hotel rooms rather than in private residences (Bruckert, Parent, and Robitaille 2003; O'Doherty 2011; Parent and Bruckert 2005).

Finally, whereas the in-call sector of the sex industry is more secure than other labour arrangements,[17] the legal context in which the workers labour increases their vulnerability. The law inadvertently affords customers a tactic for coercing workers into providing services that they do not wish to offer (such as full sexual services) or services that may endanger them (such as sex without a condom). Sex workers who participated in our research (Bruckert, Parent, and Robitaille 2003; Parent and Bruckert 2005) told us that customers can (and do) threaten that they will inform the police about the bawdy-house. Workers take this threat seriously – they are aware that the police are likely to respond to a citizen complaint (especially if it includes some suggestion, fabricated or not, that underage women are providing sexual services); customers may very well appreciate that because the law stipulates that one must be found in the bawdy-house in order to be charged, they can lay such a complaint without risking any legal repercussions for themselves.

The tension outlined in this chapter is at the heart of the ruling by Justice Himel of the Ontario Superior Court (2010 ONSC 4264) that key sections of Canada's prostitution laws (the bawdy-house provision, living on the avails of prostitution, and the communicating provision[18]) contravene section 7 of the Canadian Charter of Rights and Freedoms, which guarantees the right to "life, liberty and security of the person," and are therefore unconstitutional. The Appeal Court justices were, like Justice Himel, "satisfied that the current legal regime, and specifically the challenged *Criminal Code* provisions, interferes with prostitutes' security of the person" (ONCA 186 para. 135), although they did not agree that *Criminal Code* section 213 was unconstitutional. Justice MacPherson, writing for the minority, explained, "My colleagues recognize, correctly, that the effects of two *Criminal Code* provisions that prevent indoor prostitutes' safety measures are grossly disproportionate. I regret that they do not reach the same conclusion with respect to a third provision that has a devastating impact on the right to life and security of the person of the most vulnerable affected group, street prostitutes" (ONCA 186 para. 373).

Exclusion from Labour and Human Rights Protection

As previously noted, the labour structure of sex workers who work for or with third parties is similar to that of service sector workers in the new economy; at the same time, the criminalization of aspects of their labour complicates their work and undermines sex workers' access to labour rights. Unlike traditional employees, for instance, these workers are not able to take advantage of the provisions of the *Employment*

Insurance Act. Nor are they protected by provincial legislation such as the *Act Respecting Occupational Health and Safety* and the *Act Respecting Industrial Accidents and Occupational Diseases*. Moreover, for workers in the sex industry, the marginal and illicit status of their labour site (the bawdy-house provision, CC s. 210) or agency (under the procuring/living on the prevails provision, CC s. 212(1)) de facto restricts their access to strategies to improve their labour situation, such as unionization, formation of professional associations, and recourse to human rights acts. This context necessarily increases the potential for labour site abuse and exploitation (see also Chapter 2). It also effectively denies workers police protection. It is to this issue that we now turn.

Lack of Police Protection

The ability to call on the police for protection or for criminal justice redress, a right that most Canadians take for granted, is, in practice if not in principle, denied to sex workers. Street-based workers report that police officers are often negligent, either failing to respond to complaints of violence against sex workers or not adequately investigating violent incidents (see Bruckert and Chabot 2010; Jeffrey and MacDonald 2006). In this context of police unprofessionalism and negligence (and, as noted above, police brutality), it is not surprising that street-based sex workers do not (in general) perceive the police to be a resource, nor do they consider the officers to be operating in the sex workers' best interests. Interestingly, several of the workers who participated in our research did speak about their positive interactions with *individual* police officers who were helpful, respectful, and, sometimes, even kind; however, these officers were clearly understood to be the exception (see Bruckert, Parent, and Pouliot 2006; Parent and Bruckert 2006).

Moreover, many sex workers in all three sectors are unwilling to turn to the police for help due to their vulnerability to criminalization. In-call workers report that they are fearful of being charged under *Criminal Code* section 210(b) and also do not wish to have their employer charged under section 210(a) (out of loyalty, a sense of fairness, and/or a desire to protect their place of employment). Nor would they be willing to report to the police any violence perpetrated against them by aggressive customers. In short, these adults, who are providing consensual sexual services to other consenting adults are, in practice, unable to call on the police to protect them against harassers or aggressors (Bruckert, Parent, and Robitaille 2003; see also Bruckert and Chabot 2010; Jeffrey and MacDonald 2006; Lewis and Shaver 2006; Pivot 2002, 2004, 2006).

As we have seen, the particular criminalized nature of the industry has profound implications. Rather than protecting sex workers, the laws and their enforcement operate against sex workers' interests and constrain their ability to work in safety (see Bruckert and Chabot 2010; Bruckert and Parent 2006a; Currie and Gillies 2006; HIV/AIDS Legal Network 2005; Lewis and Shaver 2006; Parent and Bruckert 2005). Their vulnerability undermines their ability to employ strategies that would increase their security, especially in the case of street-based workers. *Criminal Code* section 210 prohibits workers from labouring in indoor venues and enjoying the measure of security that this offers (familiarity with the environment, the presence of others, alarm systems, regulated access). Moreover, in the more secure in-call sector, the threat of criminalization renders workers vulnerable to coercive tactics by customers and undermines their access to legislative labour protection. Finally, unlike workers in other sectors of the labour market, sex workers (regardless of industry sector) are hesitant to turn to the police when they have been victimized (Bruckert, Parent, and Robitaille 2003; see also Bruckert and Chabot 2010; Jeffrey and MacDonald 2006; Lewis and Shaver 2006; Pivot 2002, 2004, 2006).

Stigmatization

Sex workers must contend with a range of myths and misconceptions perpetuated by the media (see Hallgrimsdottir, Phillips, and Benoit 2006; Jeffrey and MacDonald 2006; Lowman 2000), the police, and special-interest groups such as anti-prostitution feminists and residents' associations. Common stereotypes include the assumption that sex workers are immoral, promiscuous, addicted to drugs, responsible for the transmission of STIs, dishonest and disreputable, and/or trapped in the industry, and that they are victims operating without choice (Bruckert and Chabot 2010). This stigmatization is at the root of the "discourse of disposal" (Lowman 2000) and, ultimately, the violence that workers experience. Because sex workers are constructed as unworthy and as simultaneously responsible (for their plight) and irresponsible (as social actors) by the police, the media, politicians, and the general public, acts of violence are not properly investigated/handled by authorities and there is limited media attention, little public outrage, minimal police response (as we have already seen), and negligible political will to change. It is precisely this context that allows aggressors to assault sex workers with impunity. We need look no further than the disturbing testimony presented to the 2012 Missing Women Inquiry into the police response to the murders of women from Vancouver's Downtown Eastside to appreciate that police, political, media, and public indifference is complicit in the murder of more than fifty women (see the Introduction to this book).

The consequences of working in the sex industry extend beyond the work site. We now turn to the implications of the whore stigma and the criminalization of partners to draw attention to the extra-labour implications of participation in the sex industry. Stigma is experientially real for sex workers. Many tell of being discriminated against on the basis of their occupation and of having to cope with people's assumptions that their labour is *who they are* rather than (one aspect of) *what they do*. They cite a multitude of situational examples of such discrimination: having their children forcibly removed from their care, being denied jobs when potential employers find out about their current or former labour in the sex industry, being refused apartments or evicted from their residence, being denied services by social service providers, being rejected by family members, and having their bank loan applications declined (Bruckert and Chabot 2010; Jeffrey and MacDonald 2006; Parent and Bruckert 2006; Pivot 2004). It is perhaps self-evident but nonetheless worth noting that not only are these experiences extremely stressful (and the workers explicitly identified them as such) but the fear of being stigmatized adds an additional level of strain to these individuals' private and professional lives.

Although the process of stigmatization is common, its nature, sources, and experience are varied, as stigma is necessarily conditioned by other social, economic, labour, and personal factors. That is, the stigma experienced by individuals is shaped by the intersection of the "sex worker" stigma with other elements such as gender, sexual orientation, ethnicity, class location, and other identities. At the same time, we must recognize that some sex workers are marginal individuals who are also stigmatized on the basis of other aspects of their lives. For example, some of the street-based sex workers who participated in our research spoke of being rejected, being marginalized, and experiencing prejudice because they are sex workers, and/or homeless, and/or poor, and/or lacking in cultural and social resources, and/or substance users (Parent and Bruckert 2006; see also Benoit and Millar 2001; Bruckert and Parent 2006a, 2006b; Jeffrey and MacDonald 2006; Parent and Bruckert 2005; Pivot 2004). In short, they confront intersecting stigmas that further exacerbate the marginalization, social judgment, and exclusion that they experience as sex workers.

The experience of stigma is also shaped by an individual's access to resources to mediate the stigma, resist the subtext, or manage information. Street-based sex workers, by virtue of their visibility to the public, have a limited ability to control the flow of information about their labour. By contrast, in-call and out-call workers, whose labour is more hidden, are, to a greater or lesser extent, positioned to engage in information-management strategies and hence are able to limit the stigma that they confront in their personal and professional lives. In-call workers' identity is most protected, particularly if the establishment allows workers to view potential clients prior to opening the door. Agency workers (for out-call) also have a measure of protection, as the agency will usually, as a safety precaution, verify the identity of a client prior to sending the worker. Independent in-call or out-call workers, who also generally confirm the identity of a client prior to the appointment, are, however, vulnerable to being identified by virtue of their Internet advertisements (despite attempts to disguise themselves) (Bruckert, Parent, and Pouliot 2006; Bruckert, Parent, and Robitaille 2003).

Workers who, because of the way their labour is organized, can "closet" (conceal) their labour location are able, to a greater or lesser extent, to shield themselves from moralistic judgments in their private lives; however, this practice is not without negative implications. First, as research on gay men and women has demonstrated, managing identity in this manner can be highly stressful; certainly, keeping an aspect of one's life, be it sexual orientation or occupational location, hidden from significant others and acquaintances not only is personally disorienting but also demands continual vigilance (Cain 1991). Closeted sex workers are forced to monitor their talk and behaviour, create fictions (including a job that does not exist), and avoid discussions about work to guard against disclosure. Second, fearful of having their labour location detected, they may forgo association with other sex industry workers and thereby deny themselves the support of "insiders." Finally, their hidden identity may make them vulnerable, as such information can be employed as a control strategy, by, for example, an abusive partner, a human smuggler, or a disgruntled customer. In practice, what we find is that many in-call and out-call workers seek a personally comfortable position on the spectrum between total disclosure and total concealment.

It should be noted that the experience of stigmatization is not restricted to the workers themselves but may also be a "courtesy stigma" (Goffman 1963, 28), affecting those associated with the worker (including family, friends, and partners). Moreover, the experience of being stigmatized does not end when the worker leaves the industry. The common designation of "ex" or "former" that characterizes the presentation of individuals (by the media, in particular) who at one time worked in the sex industry speaks to the enduring significance afforded the labour location. This is an ongoing concern for both current workers and those who have left the industry. Of course, individuals who have had the sex worker label more or less permanently affixed in a criminal record (and perhaps through licensing) are particularly vulnerable to the effects of enduring stigma (see Bruckert 2012; Parent and Bruckert 2006; Bruckert, Parent, and Pouliot 2006).

Conclusion

In this chapter, we used a labour lens informed by criminology to consider sex work as a form of marginalized, stigmatized, and criminalized work. This approach has allowed us to examine labour structure and process while attending to specificity, and thereby to counteract the tendency to unquestioningly conflate divergent labour practices on the basis of "moral transgression." We have also considered the implications of the particular socio-legal context of the labour, and it is to this that our final comments are directed.

There is a wealth of solid empirical research on the Canadian sex industry that has consistently demonstrated that sex workers in this country experience outrageously high levels of violence (see, for example, Benoit and Millar 2001; Bruckert and Chabot 2010; Bruckert, Parent, and Pouliot 2006; Jeffrey and MacDonald 2006; Lewis and Shaver 2006; Lowman 2000; Lowman and Fraser 1996; Parent and Bruckert 2006; Pivot 2002, 2004, 2006). Workers are victimized by clients, aggressors, community members, and the police. Sex work is not, however, *inherently* more dangerous than other comparable jobs, and sex workers are not *inherently* at risk of victimization. We know that work can endanger workers; in fact, "According to data collected by the Association of Workers Compensation Boards of Canada ... there were nearly five work-related deaths per working day" (Sharpe and Hardt 2006, 3). We also know that the nature of the risk posed by the labour site is conditioned by the particular context; workers labouring in mines, quarries, and oil wells are much more likely to experience work-related fatal violence then are workers in the finance and insurance sectors (Sharpe and Hardt 2006, 35). There is an important caveat, though: sex workers, like others who work alone, with strangers, and carry cash (such as taxi drivers and late-night store clerks) are more vulnerable to *criminal intent* violence than are workers in other labour arrangements (Leblanc and Barling 2004).

If we have learned anything from victimization studies, it is that targeted violence can be understood only in relation to the particular social, political, and legal context in which it occurs. For sex workers, this context includes a range of intersecting factors, including the "discourse of disposal" (Lowman 2000), moralistic judgments, and stigmatizing assumptions. It also includes an ambiguous legal situation: sex workers are *criminalized* for providing consensual sexual services – something that *is not criminal*. This ambiguous situation does not, of course, define the reality of sex work; it does, however, condition it. It has very real and multifaceted consequences for workers. Of particular concern is that, in practice, the criminalized context renders workers *more* vulnerable to sexual, physical, and economic violence; undermines their strategies to work safely; prohibits them from working in relatively secure indoor locations; undermines their ability to negotiate labour conditions with their employer; excludes them from accessing their human and labour rights; denies them police protection; and excludes them from judicial avenues of redress. The current law is not solely responsible for denying the human, labour, and social rights to which sex workers, like all workers in Canada, are entitled, but it is certainly complicit in denying those rights to sex workers.

Notes

1 For more information on criminalization, see Chapter 2. For more information on marginalization and stigmatization of sex work, see Benoit and Millar (2001), Bruckert (2012), Jeffrey and MacDonald (2006), Parent and Bruckert (2005, 2006), and Pivot (2004).

2 We have undertaken a number of qualitative empirical studies on different sex-work sectors, based on sociology of work categories and a feminist approach. Interviews were conducted with social actors directly involved in the targeted sectors. We conducted fourteen interviews with sex workers in massage parlours and erotic establishments in the Toronto and Montreal regions (Bruckert, Parent, and Robitaille 2003; Parent and Bruckert 2005); forty-five interviews with escorts (men, women, and transsexuals) and thirty interviews with escorts' customers (these interviews are currently being analyzed); nineteen interviews with street-based sex workers in the Ottawa-Gatineau region (Bruckert, Parent, and Pouliot 2006; Parent and Bruckert 2006); and twenty-four interviews with erotic dancers (Bruckert and Parent 2006b, 2007).

3 According to Statistics Canada, in 2007, 94.5 percent of all "prostitution"-related charges were labelled "prostitution other." The figures for 2006 and 2005 were 93.6 percent and 94.7 percent, respectively (Statistics Canada 2005a, 2006b). Statistics Canada's classification "prostitution other" seems to be limited to *Criminal Code* charges under section 213. This means that it excludes charges under sections 210 and 211 (regarding bawdy-houses) and sections 212, 170, and 171 (procuring).

4 The Parliamentary Subcommittee on Solicitation Laws concluded that street-based sex work represents only 5 to 20 percent of the industry in Canada (Subcommittee on Solicitation Laws 2006, 5).

5 Street-based sex workers also adapt their fees to the current rates for a service. They thus avoid price-busting, which can have a negative impact on the income of all workers (Parent and Bruckert 2006). See also Maloney (2004, 44).

6 Many scenarios are possible. Most in-call workers are on-site (although, in certain cases, they may be on call). Most out-call workers are on call, but some are supposed to wait for calls at the agency and travel by company car that transports several workers at a time (Parent and Bruckert 2005). See also Stella (2009).

7   Proportions may vary depending on region and other factors. Benoit and Millar (2001, 43) report that in- and out-call workers in Victoria, British Columbia, receive 78 percent of their receipts, whereas Jeffrey and MacDonald (2006, 25) indicate that in Atlantic Canada workers keep, in general, only 44 percent of their receipts.

8   Of course, not all managers are concerned with the safety of their workers. Some offer little or no protection to their "employees," and others pressure them to take risks (especially in terms of service provision) (Benoit and Millar 2001).

9   For an excellent analysis of media presentation of the sex industry, see the chapter "The Whore Stigma and the media" in Jeffrey and MacDonald (2006). On the media, see also Hallgrimsdottir, Phillips, and Benoit (2006); Lowman (2000); and Van Brunschot, Sydie, and Krull (1999).

10   On skills, see also Jeffrey and MacDonald 2006; Law 2011; Stella 2009; and sex workers' autobiographies in Van der Meulen, Durisin, and Love 2013 and in Johnson 2002.

11   As Patrice Corriveau writes in Chapter 2, although in Canada selling sexual services is not a criminal act, a number of sex-work activities are criminalized. It is important to recognize that sex workers are not subject only to arrest for activities linked to "prostitution." The police may use a number of other laws against them, including those forbidding indecent acts in public (section 173.1 of the *Criminal Code*), loitering (section 175.1a of the *Criminal Code*), and vagrancy (section 179.1a). Furthermore, the police and local politicians use other tactics to control sex workers. Notable examples include the Cyclope project in Montreal (instituted in 2002), which encourages residents to report to the police the presence of sex workers soliciting customers in their neighbourhood; in Ottawa, the community crime-prevention campaign through which owners of vehicles found driving in the sex workers' zone are not arrested but receive an official "Dear John letter" from the police department, warning them of the consequences of sex work and including (erroneous) information on sexually transmitted diseases (Ottawa Police Services 2008); and the "Safer Communities and Neighbourhood" Acts adopted by Manitoba, Yukon, Nova Scotia, Saskatchewan, and Ontario, allowing for the closure of buildings and properties in response to (in some cases anonymous) complaints.

12   High levels of violence are also found in other countries that criminalize the sex industry, such as Great Britain (McKeganey and Barnard 1996; Sanders 2004, 2005).

13   This issue is raised in a number of studies of street-based sex work (Bruckert, Parent, and Pouliot 2006; Jeffrey and MacDonald 2006; Lewis and Shaver 2006; Parent and Bruckert 2006) and is particularly well developed in Bruckert and Chabot (2010).

14   Sex workers report that they are even sometimes accosted while they go about their daily business – for example, when they are shopping at the local convenience store (Bruckert, Parent, and Pouliot 2006; Parent and Bruckert 2006). See also Jeffrey and MacDonald (2006); Lowman (2000); Maloney (2004).

15 The distinction between situational and predatory violence is not unique to the sex industry. For example, when an individual enters a financial institution with the intention of robbing the bank, we think of this person not as a customer but as a bank robber who may initially present himself as a customer to gain entry. By contrast, it is also possible to envision a situation in which a bank customer, perhaps enraged by the poor performance of his investments, becomes violent.

16 Police overwhelmingly target street-based workers. Because out-call workers are more likely to be arrested, they more often find themselves in contact with the police than do in-call workers. In our research (Bruckert, Parent, and Robitaille 2003; Parent and Bruckert 2005), one of the two women arrested and charged under section 210 mentioned the lack of respect, but also that she felt as if the officers who arrested her were acting like voyeurs.

17 Indeed, even access to informally managed indoor spaces increases the safety of street-based sex workers (Krusi et al. 2012).

18 *Criminal Code* sections 210, 212.1(j), and 213(1), respectively.

References

Abel, Gillian, Lisa Fitzgerald, and Cheryl Brunton. 2008. *The Impact of the Prostitution Reform Act on the Health and Safety Practices of Sex Workers.* Christchurch: Prostitution Law Review Committee.

Benoit, Cecilia, and Alison Millar. 2001. *Dispelling Myths and Understanding Realities: Working Conditions, Health Status, and Exiting Experiences of Sex Workers.* British Columbia: Prostitutes, Education, Empowerment and Resource Society (PEERS).

Bruckert, Chris. 2012. Stigmatized Labour: Negotiating the Mark at Work. In *Stigma Revisited: Negotiations, Resistance and the Implications of the Mark Series,* ed. Stacey Hannem and Chris Bruckert, 55-79. Ottawa: University of Ottawa Press.

Bruckert, Chris, and Fred Chabot. 2010. *Challenges: Ottawa Area Sex Workers Speak Out.* Ottawa: POWER.

Bruckert, Chris, and Tuulia Law. 2013. *Beyond Pimps, Procurers and Parasites: Mapping Third Parties in the In-call/Out-call Sex Industry.* Ottawa: Management in the Sex and Adult Industry Project.

Bruckert, Chris, and Colette Parent. 2006a. The In-call Sex Industry: Classed and Gendered Labour on the Margins. In *Criminalizing Women: Gender and (in)Justice in Neo-liberal Times,* ed. Gillian Balfour and Elizabeth Comack, 95-112. Halifax: Fernwood.

–. 2006b. *Ottawa-area Erotic Dancers: A Labour Needs Assessment (Analysis Component).* Ottawa: Status of Women Canada.

–. 2007. La danse érotique comme métier à l'ère de la vente de soi. *Cahiers de recherche sociologique* 43: 91-109.

Bruckert, Chris, Colette Parent, and Daniel Pouliot. 2006. *How To Respond to the Needs of Street Sex Workers in the Ottawa-Gatineau Region.* Ottawa: Status of Women Canada.

Bruckert, Chris, Colette Parent, and Pascale Robitaille. 2003. *Établissements de services érotiques/danses érotiques: deux formes de travail marginalisé.* Ottawa: Commission du droit du Canada.

Cain, Roy. 1991. Stigma Management and Gay Identity Development. *Social Work* 36 (1): 67-73.

Cler-Cunningham, Leonard, and Christine Christensen. 2001. *Violence Against Women in Vancouver's Street Level Sex Trade and the Police Response.* Vancouver: Ministry of Status for Women, Attorney General, and B.C. Ministry for Women's Equality.

Currie, Nora, and Kara Gillies. 2006. *Bound by the Law: How Canada's Protectionist Policies in the Areas of Both Rape and Prostitution Limit Women's Choices, Agency and Activities.* Unpublished manuscript, funded by Status of Women Canada.

Goffman, Erving. 1963. *Stigma: Management of a Spoiled Identity.* Englewood Cliffs: Prentice-Hall.

Hallgrimsdottir, Helga Kristin, Rachel Phillips, and Cecilia Benoit. 2006. Fallen Women and Rescued Girls: Social Stigma and Media Narratives of the Sex Industry. *Canadian Review of Sociology and Anthropology, Special Issue: Casting a Critical Lens on the Sex Industry in Canada* 43 (3): 265-80.

HIV/AIDS Legal Network. 2005. *Sex, Work, Rights: Reforming Canadian Criminal Laws on Prostitution.* Toronto: Canadian HIV/AIDS Legal Network.

Jeffrey, Leslie Ann, and Gayle MacDonald. 2006. *Sex Workers in the Maritimes Talk Back.* Vancouver: UBC Press.

Johnson, Merri Lisa, ed. 2002. *Jane Sexes It Up.* New York: Thunder's Mouth Press.

Krusi, Andrea, Jill Chettiar, Janice Abbott, Stefanie Strathdee, and Kate Shannon. 2012. Negotiating Safely and Sexual Risk Reduction with Clients in Unsanctioned Safer Indoor Sex Work Environments: A Qualitative Study. *American Journal of Public Health* 102 (6): 1154-59.

Law, Tuulia. 2011. Not a Sob Story. Unpublished master's thesis, University of Ottawa.

Leblanc, Murielle, and J. Barling. 2004. Understanding the Many Faces of Workplace Violence. In *Counterproductive Work Behavior: Investigations of Actors and Targets,* ed. Suzy Fox and P. Spector, 41-63. Washington, DC: APA Publishing.

Lewis, Jacqueline, and Frances Shaver. 2006. *Safety, Security and the Well-Being of Sex Workers: A Report Submitted to the House of Commons Subcommittee on Solicitation Laws.* Windsor: Sex Trade Advocacy and Research.

Lowman, John. 2000. Violence and the Outlaw Status of (Street) Prostitution in Canada. *Violence Against Women* 6 (9): 987-1011.

Lowman, John, and Laura Fraser. 1996. Violence against Persons Who Prostitute: The Experience in British Columbia. *Technical Report N. TR1996-14.* Ottawa: Department of Justice Canada.

Maloney, Emma. 2004. Beyond Survival Sex. Unpublished master's thesis, University of Ottawa, Criminology.

McKeganey, N., and M. Barnard. 1996. *Sexwork on the Streets: Prostitutes and Their Clients*. Buckingham: Open University Press.

Norwegian Working Group. 2004. *Purchasing Sexual Services in Sweden and the Netherlands*. Oslo: Ministry of Justice and the Police.

O'Doherty, Tamara. 2011. Vicitimization in Off-Street Sex Industry. *Violence Against Women* 20 (10): 1-20.

Ottawa Police Services. 2008. *Community Safety Letters*, http://www.ottawapolice. ca/Libraries/Reports_Forms_Etc/Community_safety_letter-sample_Eng.sflb.ashx.

Parent, Colette, and Chris Bruckert. 2005. Le travail du sexe dans les établissements de services érotiques: une forme de travail marginalisé. *Déviance et Société* 29 (1): 33-54.

–. 2006. Répondre aux besoins des travailleuses du sexe de rue: un objectif qui passe par la décriminalisation de leur activité de travail. *Reflets* 11: 112-45.

Penney, Jennifer. 1983. *Hard Earned Wages: Women Fighting for Better Work*. Toronto: Women's Press.

Phillips, P. 1997. Labour in the New Canadian Political Economy. In *Understanding Canada: Building the New Canadian Political Economy*, ed. Clement Wallace, 64-84. Montreal: McGill-Queen's University Press.

Pivot. 2002. *To Serve and Protect: A Report on Policing in Vancouver's Downtown East-side*. Vancouver: Pivot Legal Society.

– 2004. *Voices for Dignity: A Call to End the Harms Caused by Canada's Sex Trade Laws*. Vancouver: Pivot Legal Society.

–. 2006. *Beyond Decriminalization: Sex Work, Human Rights and a New Framework for Law Reform*. Vancouver: Pivot Legal Society, www.pivotlegal.org/pdfs/ BeyondDecrimLongReport.pdf.

Ritzer, George. 2004. *The McDonaldization of Society*. Thousand Oaks: Pine Forge Press.

Sanders, Teela. 2004. The Risks of Street Prostitution: Punters, Policy and Protesters. *Urban Studies* 41 (9): 1703-17.

–. 2005. *Sex Work: Risky Business*. Devon: Willan Publishing.

Sharpe, Andrew, and Jill Hardt. 2006. *Five Deaths a Day: Workplace Fatalities in Canada 1993-2005*. Ottawa: Centre for the Study of Living Standards.

Statistics Canada. 2005a. *Uniform Crime Reporting Survey*. Ottawa: Statistics Canada.

–. 2005b. *Women in Canada: A Gender-based Statistical Report*. Ottawa: Ministry of Industry.

–. 2006a. *Measuring Violence Against Women*. Ottawa: Statistics Canada.

–. 2006b. *Uniform Crime Reporting Survey*. Ottawa: Statistics Canada.

–. 2007. *Uniform Crime Reporting Survey*. Ottawa: Statistics Canada.

Stella. 2009. Working Conditions Special. *Constellation*, April.

Subcommittee on Solicitation Laws of the House of Commons. 2006. *The Challenge of Change: A Study of Canada's Criminal Prostitution Laws*. Ottawa: House of Commons.

Van Brunschot, Erin Gibbs, Rosalind A. Sydie, and Catherine Krull. 1999. Images of Prostitution: The Prostitute and Print Media. *Women and Criminal Justice* 10 (4): 47-72.

Van der Meulen, Emily, Elya M. Durisin, and Victoria Love, eds. 2013. *Selling Sex: Experience, Advocacy, and Research on Sex Work in Canada.* Vancouver: UBC Press.

The Idea of Community and Collective Action

Reflections on Forum XXX

MARIA NENGEH MENSAH

4

I'm a holistic health professional, Your Honour!

— KARA GILLIES 2006, 75

Please don't rescue me!

— PING PONG 2006, 51

This chapter focuses on *Forum XXX: Celebrating a Decade of Action – Designing Our Future,* a congress that brought together an international community of female sex workers at the Université du Québec à Montréal, 18-22 May 2005 (Cantin et al. 2006). The emergence and visibility of this international mobilization sent shock waves through the social field, as "prostitutes" came out as organized social actors who, stimulated by the fight against HIV/AIDS, consolidated a community approach that takes a new view of sex work. This new visibility brings forth new discourse from sex workers and creates a breach in the current dominant prohibitionist or neo-abolitionist discourse.

This forum for sex workers was organized by three groups celebrating a tenth anniversary – Stella (Montreal, Canada), Cabiria (Lyon, France), and the Durbar Mahila Samanwaya Committee (Calcutta, India). As the project took shape, more than fifty other groups were added to the list of participating organizations (see the appendix to this chapter). Ultimately, 250 individuals with experience in sex work or involved in offering services to sex workers, along with their allies, gathered to exchange information and discuss respective experiences, common issues, and action strategies. Forum XXX provided a means to counter marginalization by "channelling the voices and words of thousands of sex workers, members of our organizations on five continents ... voices from India, France, Sweden, Thailand, Argentina, New Zealand, Israel, South Africa, Hong Kong, the United States, Canada, Quebec and more" (Cantin et al. 2006, 131).

The historic event, unprecedented in Canada, privileged discussion, reflection, and sharing of support strategies for sex workers all over the world.[1] Policies and community support measures by and for sex workers were consolidated, and the stigma that affects sex workers – the myth that prostitutes are dangerous vamps and vectors of disease – was addressed. Forum XXX's objectives were attained: together, participants took stock of the sex workers' movement, developed a shared vision of actions undertaken regarding the HIV/AIDS pandemic, and formulated strategies for the future.

The recent attack on sex work insists on discrediting not only the organizations that defend the rights of people who perform sex work and demand decriminalization but also the spokespersons for these organizations.[2] As one participant at Forum XXX observed,

> Some people think we're a bunch of idiots, quasi-intellectuals, elitists who don't know what we're talking about. But we come from the front lines, we work on the front lines and we spend time there every day. So clearly we're well placed to know that life ain't always a rose garden. Nor is everything black and white – there are lots of grey zones. (Thiboutot 2006b, 24)

For instance, in May 2005 the feminist Web site Sisyphe.org sent a letter to the electronic media to protest against the use of money "from the funds for the fight against AIDS" to organize Forum XXX. In the view of Mélina Bernier (2007, 98, our translation), these abolitionist feminists "called the event illegitimate and accused its organizers of being opportunistic and complicit with the sex industry and with patriarchy" – a charge amounting to defamation of one of the organizers:

> Stella is not fighting HIV/AIDS, it is promoting the rights of *a minority of female prostitutes,* who claim to speak on behalf of the majority and trivialize the sexual exploitation of women by propagating the lie that prostitution is, for the majority, a "freely chosen" occupation. This ideology conceals the sexual relations of domination at the core of the institution of prostitution. (Carrier 2005, emphasis in original, our translation)

In addition to ignoring the social and health-related expertise developed by Stella, these anti-prostitution feminists assume that no woman in her right mind would voluntarily perform sex work. Some even say that when female sex workers claim the notion of consent – and the freedom to do what they want with their bodies – this is "hijacking feminist demands and a disconnection from [feminism's] emancipatory aim" (Poulin 2008, 402, our translation). Thus, the indignation of anti-prostitution authors resonates in popular opinion and is reflected in common sense. It is unthinkable that someone would want another human being to be assaulted and exploited. Yet the abolitionist analysis is based on a *total incomprehension of the idea of community* among sex workers, and thus of their organizations, their collective actions, and the resulting discourse:

> One of the major consequences of abolitionism is that the words of sex workers are invalidated, and as a result, so is any form of collective action they may undertake. Sex workers constitute one of society's most silenced groups. Their words are rarely produced, rarely listened to; their statements are constantly weighed against people's suspicions of manipulation or alienation. (Monnet 2006a, 87)

In fact, as we shall see below, for many sex workers, the experience of sex work is neither an intrinsic quality nor an absolute and definitive life experience. We will also understand that representatives of sex-worker–driven organizations are social actors, the catalysts for change.

Analyzing Sex-Worker–Driven Activism

In this chapter, I analyze the discourse and actions embedded in Forum XXX in light of the notion of "sexual community," formulated by Jeffrey Weeks (2000). For the gay and lesbian movement, Weeks explains how this notion aptly describes the context within which it is possible to articulate an identity and values for the development of a way of life, as well as margins of manoeuvre and options for collective action. This notion, in Weeks's (2000, 182) view, facilitates comprehension of social movements and political campaigns, linked to sexuality, that challenge the established order. The context for emergence of the movement that interests us here, however, involves a community that is based not on sexual identity, as is the gay and lesbian community, but on the identity of the sex worker.

I suggest that the constitutive categories that define Weeks's notion of sexual community make it possible to understand the activism and voice of sex workers: nude dancers, escorts, webmasters, telephone operators, actresses, "prostitutes," dominatrixes, independent or working in an establishment, migrant or not, self-employed or working for an employer. Furthermore, I argue that in seeking to redefine the identity of the individuals concerned by this community, by articulating an ethics of internal and external openness, and by laying the groundwork for a critical social movement, the spokespersons for sex workers' organizations help to broaden our thinking about sexuality as a driving force for collective action. This is why, for a number of reasons, sex workers form a unique community.

What Makes Sex Workers a Community?

Considering sex workers to be a community presupposes that there is a sort of unity among them. Iris Marion Young (1990) emphasizes that although the *ideal* of community is often necessary for taking action, this ideal is problematic because it evokes an unrealistic, homogeneous vision of the groups involved. In fact, this is a common pitfall.

The differences among individual women, men, and transgender persons who do sex work are well known. For example, studies on female sex workers and their working and living conditions are conducted from a feminist angle, whereas research on male (Dorais 2003), trans, and intersexed (Namaste 2000, 2005) sex workers are, regrettably, almost never the subject of feminist analysis. Furthermore, there are many differences among individuals of a given sex or gender who perform sex work, depending on the sector, the type of activity, the services offered, and the clienteles served. There are also differences according to the individual positioning of each worker with regard to racialization, ethnicity, social class, sexual preference, age, physical and intellectual capacities, and experiences with violence. Some identify themselves as feminists, whereas others are frightened by this word, if only because it is associated with anti-prostitution and abolitionist discourse. Between richer and poorer, Canadians and Americans, Europeans and Asians, urban and rural, right wing and left wing, the experiences are both numerous and varied. In fact, there is no reason to believe that sex workers have other experiences in common. Yet, on the collective level, two constants cut across their experience of sex work: stigmatization and the desire to take concerted action.

Stigmatization

The whore stigma is certainly the strongest tie binding the members of this community. The experience of sex work is rife with confrontation with stereotypes linked to sex and gender; discriminatory application of laws; criminalization or entry into the judicial system; rejection by the feminist movement; and precarious working conditions that often affect workers' health, safety, and dignity. As one Forum XXX participant noted, "We are a community because it gives us strength, we share a particular sex worker culture, we are all away from our home communities and we are looked down on by mainstream society" (Ping Pong 2006, 51).

The manifestations of this stigma are both direct (in barriers to access to social, health, legal, and police services) and indirect (prejudice or mistrust by family and friends; inimical laws and policies).[3] The police, anti-prostitution feminists, the media, and the general public exacerbate this stigmatization. Sex workers themselves also feed it through certain internal divisions – between HIV seropositive and seronegative workers, for example, or between nude dancers and street-based workers, or between those working in their home country and illegal migrant workers. We could call this interiorized stigma.

> The stigmatization of prostitution creates a pseudo-hierarchy of types of work and types of workers, which can be very divisive. It can also lead people to distance themselves from the issues pertinent to some sex workers – for example, drug use, street work, migrant work, race issues or gender issues. Such separation creates tensions, and some groups of sex workers feel especially excluded because of these divides. (Participants in Forum XXX 2006b, 75)

During the final plenary session of Forum XXX, the participants emphasized that stigmatization is, by far, the most important and the most negative experience that they have. All sex workers experience it, making it a collective problem:

> The heavy stigma attached to sex work often stands in the way of our ability to take pride in ourselves and in our work. Negative stereotypes that misrepresent who we are can make it difficult to come out publicly and shine in all our diversity ... Often, our strategies for creating positive images are met with the criticism that we are overglamourizing ourselves and our work. (Participants in Forum XXX 2006a, 52)

Disrepute is at the heart of the whore stigma – a social label redolent with opprobrium and contempt that discredits the individual in her interactions with others, relegating her to subnormal status. According to Erving Goffman (1963), an individual is said to be "stigmatized" when she presents an attribute that radically changes the way she perceives herself and how she is perceived by others. In this sense, stigma is a special case in the typification of difference – one that is very much in the foreground of our attention and negatively evaluated. Even the definition of the term "prostitution" is stigmatizing, explains Gail Pheterson (1996): the prostitute is, ipso facto, morally depraved, physically defective, psychologically delinquent, sexually abnormal, legally deviant or criminal, medically a vector of contagion, personally under-age, socially traumatized by violence and misery – in short, a threat to public order. So when organizations' spokespersons speak on behalf of sex workers, they refuse to adopt the dissimulation strategies used by stigmatized people – to be unseen and unheard – to hide this stigma. In the process, sex-worker advocates are even more stigmatized and cause greater discomfort, rising indignation, and stronger incomprehension.

In other words, sex work is stigmatized and criminalized because it is not the norm. But it is also on the basis of lived stigmatization that a sense of community has emerged and transcended the individual differences among the people involved. The community of sex workers is not fixed; it has many divisions. In spite of this, people who suffer the whore stigma have a sort of "diasporic" awareness through which they find themselves and recognize each other. And this feeling, this awareness, has concrete effects: the creation of discourse, the finding of a voice, and the proliferation of stories, spoken and written. This gives the community better visibility and greater "expressibility."[4] As workers at Stella note,

> Stella is for the most part made up of and managed by sex workers. It places sex workers at the heart of its outreach work and its decision-making structure – members, volunteers, employees and members of the board of directors. The way sex workers have come together within Stella has helped establish solidarity and create a space where people feel a strong sense of belonging. It has also helped sex workers to recognize and identify common concerns and needs, and to translate them into collective actions and demands. Our challenge for the future is to continue working on collective mobilization by sharing our experiences in the spirit of diversity. (Laliberté and St-Jean 2006, 45)

The Desire To Take Concerted Action

Although they come from different cultures, work in a wide variety of social and legislative contexts, and have divergent opinions or perspectives for action, sex workers throughout the world have expressed their desire to build a common front. This means more than simply acknowledging each other's opinions; it also involves planning actions aimed at harmonizing actors' interventions by integrating them into an overall strategy and, ultimately, attaining common objectives. The actors form groups, adopt common strategies, and agree to act together.

One of the earliest collective actions by Western sex workers took place in 1826, when six "prostitutes" in Verdun, France, went from the suburb to which their activity had been relegated to the centre of the town, in a parody of a religious procession, to denounce police repression and social ostracism (Merrimann 1994). In the late twentieth century, similar actions proliferated locally and internationally. In 1975, French "prostitutes" took action by occupying churches – Saint-Nizier in Lyon and Saint-Bernard in Paris – while in the United States, American "prostitutes" founded Call Off Your Old Tired Ethics (COYOTE). In 1984, the International Committee for Prostitutes' Rights, composed almost exclusively of women, sex "prostitutes" and feminists, was formed. A year later, the committee coordinated the World Whore Congress in Amsterdam, at which the participants established a "new political grammar" that placed sex workers at the centre of the discourse. The *World Charter for Prostitutes' Rights,* in which "prostitution" was defined as an income-generating activity – a "job" – was published (International Committee for Prostitutes' Rights 1985). Then, female sex workers organized in India to formulate a strategy for fighting social stigmatization; they coordinated a first national conference attended exclusively by sex workers and their children, marking the start of this marginalized group's resistance. They published the shared reflections issuing from this conference in the now-famous *Calcutta Manifesto for Sex Worker Rights* (Durbar Mahila Samanwaya Committee 2000). In 2005, the European Conference on Sex Work, Human Rights, Labour and Migration, held in Brussels, Belgium, also produced a manifesto, written and approved by 120 sex workers from twenty-six countries, listing the inequalities and injustices to which they were subjected and proposing "changes needed to create a more equitable society – one that acknowledges and values sex workers, [their] rights, and [their] labour" (International Committee on the Rights of Sex Workers in Europe 2005, 1).

Today, cooperation and collective action strategies take different forms, depending on the needs and the available resources. The creation of publishing houses, Web sites, and magazines, as well as peer health promotion, unionization, the institution of educational programs for female sex workers and their children, and the foundation of open universities are some examples of concerted actions presented at Forum XXX. Other initiatives were proposed to help female sex workers gain economic independence. Organizations and groups also developed cultural programs in which, through artistic expression – video, dance, theatre, comedy, and other kinds of performance – sex workers expressed their creativity and explored their own representations of themselves and their work. These exchanges were invaluable: "While our individual experiences may be very different, they can teach us a lot. It's important to come together and share our knowledge and expertise. Together, we have the power to make history. Together, we can fight for our economic, sexual and social autonomy" (Laliberté and St-Jean 2006, 43).

Within the community, the diversity of thought and action among different individuals and groups involved constantly poses the challenge of inclusion and solidarity. Outside of the community, another major challenge arises: making the critical field of sexuality as socioeconomic exchange a fertile ground for collective action.[5]

How Does Sexuality Drive Collective Action?

The sex workers' community channels its energy into fighting for the recognition of sex work as work and for the recognition of their human rights and of their legitimacy as workers. In doing this, the community articulates the four constitutive elements of a sexual community, as proposed by Weeks (2000): 1) community as a focus identity; 2) community as ethos or repository of values; 3) community as social capital; and 4) community as politics. The members of the sex workers' community, united in their identity as sex professionals, share values, create networks for social action and to fight for their rights, and combat discrimination through a politics of disclosure.

Organizing around a Subversive Professional Identity

As a group, sex workers have put forth a subversive professional identity because, although linked to a sort of sexual identity, they claim an identity based on an income-generating occupation in the sex industry. This is subversive precisely because sex work as work has an ideological attachment to other marginalized or atypical work. Individuals *work with* sexuality and eroticism through various practices; they use technical, interpersonal, and physical skills; they draw on capacities for intimacy, management, marketing, and promotion of their services; and they must possess an ability to cope with constant stigmatization. It is this professional sexual identity – even if it is unstable and changing (Parent 2001) – rather than personal sexual identity that brings male, female, and trans sex workers together. Sexual identity and worker identity are both subverted in the process.

It should be remembered, in passing, that this is not the first time that envisaging an invisible activity as real work has been the subject of struggle. In Quebec in the 1970s, women working in the home, led by the Association féminine d'éducation et d'action sociale, undertook studies and actions to bring to light their invisible work in the home (Bérubé-Gagné 1984). Women working with their husbands in profit-making businesses have also fought to obtain wage, social, and tax measures recognizing their "under-the-table" work (Bourdon 2004). Finally, there is the ongoing struggle of domestic workers to raise their labour out of contempt, prejudice, and clandestine exploitation (Paquet 2007). The activism of sex workers reiterates claims by all people "at the bottom of the ladder" who demand recognition of their status as workers, respect for their rights and dignity, and inclusion in labour laws and regulation. Thus, envisaging "prostitution" as work – sex work – allows for an understanding of the *common interest* that lies within the broader struggles concerning the invisibility and inferiorization of women's work, and concerning the racist and sexist exploitation at the core of capitalism.

The assignment of sexual identity linked to labour is thus opposed to the essentialism of the modern discursive construction of sexuality described by Michel Foucault (1976), through which sex becomes a core feature of human identities, and multiple discourses on the subject proliferate as truth. The common professional identity claimed by sex workers creates a major inversion, as it inscribes individuals within a sphere of legitimacy outside of themselves, while being plural (what they *do*), as a positive quality rather than an inevitable or naturalized position (what they *are*). As Weeks explains,

Movements such as these are not simply expressing a pre-existing essence of social being. Identities and belongings are being constructed in the very process of organization itself. They are effective in so far as they can speak a language which brings people into the activities, alignments and subjectivities being shaped; and the most effective language available is the language of community. (Weeks 2000, 185)

Furthermore, the identity of "sex workers" is sustained over time by activist practices and symbolic actions that reaffirm both the professional identity and the differences among individuals. This identity is expressed through annual unifying events, such as the International Sex Workers Rights Day (3 March) and the International Day to End Violence against Sex Workers (17 December). Annie Sprinkle writes:

Every year when I create or attend a gathering on December 17, it is a deeply moving experience. I take some moments to feel grateful that I worked as a prostitute for so many years and came out alive. I remember those who didn't survive and I fear for those who won't unless real changes are made – namely safer working conditions and the same police protection other citizens get without recrimination. (Sprinkle 2008)

The professional identity is also manifested by pride, a direct response to the shame produced by stigma. For instance, in describing the assets of the collective in which she is involved, a participant from India underlines the pride that she feels in having improved the status of sex workers as "working people": "We have created selfhood and self-esteem among sex workers and generated the discourse that sex work is an occupation and not a moral condition, and therefore sex workers are workers in the sex industry and not merely 'fallen' or 'aberrant' women, men or transgendered people who are entitled to a set of rights" (Debnath 2006, 29).

Another participant from Quebec, Émilie Laliberté, expressed the importance of being recognized for her work:

Before I started working at Stella, I had experienced isolation and the fear of being judged, despite the fact that I'd never felt I was doing anything bad ... quite the contrary! With my fiery tongue, I made many people happy! But in experiencing the acceptance of this wonderful community of sex workers, I finally managed to breathe deeply and feel good. For the first time in my life as an escort, I felt alive, free and happy, accepted and loved, and seen for who I am. I finally had a positive view on my work. (Laliberté and St-Jean 2006, 45)

Shared Values: Pooling of Knowledge and Respect for Diversity

According to Weeks, sexual community is also formed of a set of ethical principles. In differentiating sexual identity from professional identity, sex workers advocate a new relational philosophy. They do not so much seek to answer the existential question "How should we live?" but wonder, "How should we work?" Thus, sex workers do not demand a distinction between freely chosen sex work and situations of abuse and violence. They know that there is a difference and that the situation is terrible for those upon whom "prostitution" is imposed as servitude. In those cases, advocates no longer speak about work but about coercion and exploitation. What they want is recognition of the legitimacy of sex work, for, in their view, this legitimacy is the only possible guarantee that real and concrete means will be used to fight abuse, violence, and exploitation in every context in which sex work is practised, without distinction. This ethical principle is articulated along two axes: the sharing of knowledge and expertise developed through work, and respect for diversity and marginalities within the movement.

Two Montreal participants made the following observation about the sharing of knowledge and expertise:

And the experience of our peer outreach workers has definitely been a major element in helping us reach sex workers in Montreal and surrounding areas, and to understand their needs. At Stella, we believe that an erotic dancer is hired for the thousands of "tricks" she's learned on the job, her human relations and social skills, and because having worked with thousands of clients and all sorts of other dancers, she's a professional in her field. Recognizing that experience and giving her credit for it – that's empowerment ... Dancers, masseuses, prostitutes and escorts have all been able to share their knowledge among themselves and with a variety of their peers. And above all, they've broken their own isolation and that of the other women they rub shoulders with every day. (Laliberté and St-Jean 2006, 43)

With respect to diversity and marginalities, an inclusive, humanist, utopian vision is evoked: "We seek a world where all marginalized communities live in harmony enjoying equal respect, rights and dignity. We work to make real a social order where there is no discrimination based on race, class, creed, religion, caste, gender, occupation or disease status and all global citizens live in peace and harmony" (Debnath 2006, 30).

In Canada, the inclusion of differences among sex workers comes to the fore when the subject of foreign workers is raised, although this is not specific to the sex industry. Canadian workers want to avoid an attitude that is nationalistic or hostile to immigration: "We are however trying to be proactive, and in addition to countering some of the dominant antitrafficking discourses, we are attempting to network with both sex workers' groups and migrant workers' groups to come to some mutual agenda and understanding. Unfortunately, it's been very difficult" (Gillies 2006, 73).

The Social Capital of Resistance: Health, Safety, and Dignity

Weeks also asks us to see in the sexual liberation movements of recent decades the development of a particular social capital that defines a community. This is illustrated, in his view, by the responses of gay men to the appearance of HIV/AIDS. Directly affected by the epidemic, gay men implemented "safer sex," the objectives of which were to promote survival (of gay men), fight stigmatization, encourage community development, and raise self-esteem. At first, community links were forged in the awareness of the immediate danger, urgency, and personal threat posed by AIDS. As the pandemic spread, the gay community's engagement broadened. Gay men mobilized their resources to become frontline actors in both HIV prevention and providing support to people living with HIV/AIDS. They developed social networks of an unprecedented density and turned HIV/AIDS into an opportunity for creativity and community affirmation.

I found similar social capital in the community of sex workers, among whom community organization was also consolidated with the need to fight HIV/AIDS. Indeed, the advent of the HIV/AIDS epidemic was a key moment for the articulation of demands for healthier, safer working conditions that respect human dignity. At the time, the public authorities envisaged forcing "prostitutes" to receive medical exams and undergo compulsory HIV tests; in their view, these measures would avoid infections of their customers, who could then infect their wives, who would, in turn, transmit the virus to their children. Sex workers refused such forms of social and medical control, for there were already numerous public health measures in existence and there was little concern for the fate of the workers themselves: "We certainly had no interest in becoming the epidemic's new scapegoats. In other words, we refused to be further stigmatized, this time as 'vectors for disease transmission.' We took up our agency in preventing disease in our community" (Thiboutot 2006b, 23). They also argued that they had an interest in protecting themselves, that they had already developed strategies for protection against infections transmissible by sexual activity or by blood, and that they had to strengthen these strategies and fight the systemic barriers to their everyday living and working conditions.

Cabiria, a community-based organization in France, offers resources to sex workers with a global health perspective:

> We support sex workers as they encounter medical, administrative, legal and social services, and provide everyday help. We also welcome them into our space, which is intended to provide a friendly atmosphere and create a sense of community and closeness. As well as support and counselling, we provide legal clinics, meals, and we run a 24-hour hotline in case of violence or arrest. In addition, the association has also developed a research department, primarily in social sciences and international relations, a publishing house and a website ... Lastly, since the end of 2002, the association has taken on another innovative project, which aims to give everyone access to learning.

This endeavour was built on the model of people's universities and is open to all traditionally excluded populations. (Monnet 2006b, 33)

Israeli activist Liad Kantorowicz explained how she became involved, with the help of local stakeholders, in meeting the needs of her migrant colleagues originally from Russia: "We ran a hotline which was used by migrant sex workers. Its purpose was to help them reach accessible, non-judgmental doctors who could meet their healthcare needs without opting for formal healthcare. The sex workers were accompanied to healthcare services by Russian-speaking volunteers who provided support and mediation" (Kantorowicz 2006, 47).

Mediation starts from the following premise: health cannot be dissociated from other human rights, such as the right to safety, security, dignity, and equality. That is why the activists of the Asociación de Mujeres Meretrices de la Argentina, which represents eleven provincial organizations across Argentina, have broadened their strategy for action. Éléna Reynaga, president of the association, explains: "We decided that we could not talk about health rights when we didn't even have fundamental rights and freedoms. Therefore we started a political lobby, to organize political events in favour of decriminalization. Between the two objectives that we had been discussing, we chose to work for fundamental rights and freedoms by organizing political action at the national assembly" (Reynaga 2006, 67).

Another large collective with thousands of members preferred to highlight the health, safety, and dignity of sex workers by setting up a microcredit system and a school, both completely managed by women from within the sector: "[The Durbar Mahila Samanwaya Committee has] created environments and institutions where our children can learn, play and grow. We run two residential homes for children to provide them with educational opportunities usually denied them by 'mainstream' society, which stigmatizes our children along with us" (Debnath 2006, 30).

Finally, the participants at Forum XXX unanimously recognized the harmful effects of criminalization on access to overall health and respect for human rights. They all talked about challenges, both individual and collective, posed by laws and questions of fundamental rights.

Criminalization makes them vulnerable while legitimizing social stigmatization and discrimination (see Chapter 2):

> One of the responses that we have come up with at Maggie's [Toronto] is to insist that other social justice movements, academics and activists counter not only the criminalization and stigmatization of sex workers but also that of our clients and management. To do otherwise is highly pathologizing and buys into the false notion that the exploitation of sexual labour is somehow substantially different from, and more problematic than, the exploitation of any other form of labour, and it significantly undermines a lot of the work we have done to date to advance our social and legal standing. (Gillies 2006, 73).

> We want laws and policies that do not come from a protectionist standpoint, that do not discriminate against us or against our work, and that do not endorse the stigma against sex work. Any type of law reform must not bring with it harsher penalties than the ones that already exist – the dangers that current laws have created effectively place our lives in danger. (Participants in Forum XXX 2006c, 102)

These are the significant elements of the social capital accumulated by the sex workers' community engaged in the fight to defend rights centred on health, safety, security, and dignity.

Sexual Community as Politics: Disclosure

The fourth founding element of the community that uses *sexuality as work* as the basis for a movement promoting rights concerns the power relations engendered by its members' voices. "Coming out"[6] is an eminently political process, and the politics of disclosure are not simple:

> In response to our continuous attempts to show our diversity as sex workers, the public demands that we reveal personal information about ourselves in order to be considered credible. Yet when we do that, they discredit us by saying we are not representative of sex workers if we don't fit their stereotypes ... But regardless of where one fits

on that scale, there is definitely an emotional toll attached to coming out. (Participants in Forum XXX 2006a, 54).

Announcing aloud that one is a sex worker is a reality that is sometimes imposed, but it nevertheless symbolizes a rejection of victimization and a search for social recognition: "Putting oneself on display, for the speaker, means denouncing a problematic situation, but more generally, it means entering into a relationship of power to confront the established order" (Bernier 2007, 87, our translation). Their organizations have enabled sex workers to dismantle "existing constructs on gender, sex, sexuality and sex work" and create "spaces for the voice of the sex workers' community to be heard in the larger society" (Debnath 2006, 29). These spaces and voices underline the political significance of sex workers' disclosing their identity. They now emerge as political subjects, with new claims about sexuality as workplace.

Sex workers do not all disclose in the same way or in similar situations. The analysis of circumstances under which they disclose, who they choose to tell, and the dissimulation strategies that they implement indicate that they come out gradually and selectively. However, "Some display themselves more spontaneously," notes Mélina Bernier (2007, 88, our translation); "[f]or these people, it's a way to be activists on a daily basis, whereas others draw on their experience in more specific contexts, such as during training or an interview." The activists attending Forum XXX publicly identified themselves by various means, such as through artistic expression or participation in a demonstration, press conference, or radio or television program. Making their demands visible and audible dismantles stigma and is part of the politicization process. As one participant recounted,

In May of 2002 I first agreed to out myself publicly by getting interviewed [by the] Israeli national newspaper *Haaretz*. The article stirred up lots of public attention, as this was [the] first time that a sex worker was outing herself and referring to sex work as a source of income rather than a source of oppression. It was also the first time that the term "sex worker" was used in Hebrew, the first time that the concept of sex workers' rights were discussed, and the first time that a sex worker who does not see herself as a victim was discussing it. (Kantorowicz 2006, 48)

The politics of disclosure deconstructs the prejudices associated with the victimization of sex workers and throws into question the language used in and the moral values of society. However, there are numerous obstacles to disclosure, raised both outside and inside the workers' community,

> because of the stigmatization that taints sex work and divides female sex workers among themselves: neither all forms of sex work nor the stereotypes associated with the types of people who practice them (transsexuals, cultural minorities, migrants, students, mothers, poor people, drug users, and so on) are seen in the same way by public opinion. In short, it is not always possible to "come out" in every environment or under just any conditions. The sex workers who disclose expose themselves to violence, rejection, loss of friends, being fired, and so on. (Bernier 2007, 91, our translation)

Indeed, the participants in Forum XXX asserted that "the criminalization of our lives and work helps to keep us invisible, and that can make it tricky to come out publicly. Choosing to be visible can be problematic because of the risk of being put in jail, suffering violence or being deported" (2006a, 54). It is therefore preferable to choose the environments in which one discloses, to respect the decision of those who do not want to disclose, and to construct safe places to support the disclosure of those who are ready to come out. The positive effects of a well-prepared coming-out supported by other sex workers were evoked at Forum XXX. An alternative to shame and isolation, such a coming-out builds a sense of belonging and pride in the community. One's public testimonial as a member of a unique sexual community becomes a resource for mobilization:

> We are stronger in numbers, and with the strength of other sex workers beside you, coming out can be an easier process. When we hold

onto and internalize shame and stigma, this impacts our ability to mobilize and organize for our rights. It is difficult to build a movement and advocate for ourselves if we remain anonymous or if the burden of pushing the agenda is left to a few people. (Participants in Forum XXX 2006a, 54).

In Weeks's view, the most important aspect of judging the political effectiveness of a social movement linked to sexuality is in assessing its impact on the life of the people involved. One therefore cannot measure the "success" of a sexual community by looking only at its capacity to attain a particular objective or legislative reform, as significant as those may be. In this regard, the words of the participants in Forum XXX about what they valued about the gathering are eloquent:

Forming and supporting sex worker groups is especially important so together we have the strength and power to confront our difficulties and pursue our collective dream ... I gained a lot of knowledge and experience from this trip. I was especially aware that we share the same ideas and the same goals for our work. However we do it, wherever we do it, we are all sex workers. Whatever we strive for, if we can find common goals, then together we can succeed. (Anonymous, in Cantin et al. 2006, 115)

Thanks to you I have been able to go to university once in my life, thank you, J![7] Thanks to you, I began to exteriorize the emotions that I had inside, the right to be as I am, my choices and my convictions in life. Yes, I am one of the 250 participants and I'm proud of that (I even was congratulated by the girls where I work). Wow, what a great reward to be congratulated for my involvement by women who aren't involved. (MMJ in Cantin et al. 2006, 115, our translation)

Thank you for inspiring me to make the changes needed in my own community. Thank you for helping me to see that I myself can become the answer I constantly seek. Thank you for having rekindled the fire that lives inside me. When I think of Stella, I will always remember the press conference, when all the egos faded to the background and everyone's voices melted into a single voice. What cohesion. What power. (CC in Cantin et al. 2006, 116, our translation)

I want to thank Stella for the opportunity to visit my sex worker family. Apart from what I learned in the meeting rooms, I exchanged and learned a lot talking over lunch, in the hallways. There was something from each person and each country that were [sic] so interesting. Sometimes we understood each other, sometimes we didn't, whatever, we got warmth and support from each other anyway. Stella, you took such good care of us like real family. Thank you from the bottom of my heart. (PP, in Cantin et al. 2006, 117)

Is the Sex Workers' Community Recognized and Legitimate?

Up to this point, I have discussed how the mobilization of sex workers – the movement's ethical, social, political, and identity foundations – represents a new form of collective action for the members of this critical sexual community in Weeks's (2000) sense. But the existence of the community also depends on a public composed of interlocutors who can put themselves in "listening mode" (Toupin 2005, 81, our translation) – a receptive critical mass that confers legitimacy and recognition upon sex worker community.

In Canada, the Stella organization has received numerous awards and honourable mentions. In 1996, it received the Sécurité des femmes (Women and Safety) award from the City of Montreal's Comité d'action femmes et sécurité urbaine for its intervention tool called *Bad Tricks and Assaulters List,* which is still published every month. In 2000, the Fédération des femmes du Québec awarded Stella a Prix Idola-Saint-Jean with a special mention for audacity and determination. In 2004, the organization received the annual award for excellence in the community initiatives category from the Réseau de la santé et des services sociaux du Québec and the Quebec minister of health and social services. This award highlighted the excellence of two other tools, *Guide XXX*[8] and *Art of Striptease,* distributed to female sex workers to prevent HIV and other sexually transmitted infections, thus improving their living and working conditions and safety. Finally, Stella received the Canadian Award for Action on HIV/AIDS and Human Rights from the Canadian HIV/AIDS Legal Network and Human Rights Watch. In conferring this distinction, the Canadian HIV/AIDS Legal Network (2006) was "recognizing over a decade of courageous work defending sex workers' human rights and advocating against the criminalization of their lives and livelihood."

In Thailand, the Empower Foundation, a federation of associations driven by and for female sex workers, created in 1984, also received a number of distinctions. In 2005, the director of Empower in Chiang Mai, Pornpit Puckmai, received the first Thai National Human Rights Award for her exceptional contribution to the defence of women's rights. Preferring to share the honour with her community, Puckmai gave an eloquent acknowledgment:

> I want this award to be an inspiration to all of us sex workers fighting for our rights. I want to say to you that if you are a sex worker and you're thinking about whether to join the fight for sex worker rights then ... do it! This is recognition for all sex workers that we have rights and that we are more than capable of defending our rights. This is not just my award. This is our award. The Power We Have: The Power We Share! (Puckmai 2005).

In 2008, at the High Level Meeting on AIDS during the general meeting of the United Nations Development Program and the Joint United Nations Programme on HIV/AIDS (UNAIDS), the Empower Foundation received the prestigious Red Ribbon Award.

In India, the Durbar Mahila Samanwaya Committee has been highly praised. The "untamables'" committee (the English translation of the name), a forum composed of 65,000 sex workers in the western Bengal region, combats systemic barriers encountered by sex workers every day and manages the Sonagachi Project, a cooperative of female sex workers, founded in 1992. This cooperative is considered a best practices model by UNAIDS (Mukerjee 2006). It is recognized, notably, for having maintained the lowest HIV infection rate among participating female sex workers.

On the global scale, the Asia Pacific Network of Sex Workers received the International Award for Action on HIV/AIDS and for Human Rights from the Canadian HIV/AIDS Legal Network and Human Rights Watch for having denounced a new law that likens "prostitution" to human trafficking and casts such a wide net that simply owning condoms is cause for arrest (see Chapter 5). The social and community health contributions of a number of sex workers' groups, from all parts of the world, were recently acknowledged by the Open Society Institute (Crago 2008). Among the remarkable actions underlined are:

- Outreach in the street and in brothels, as well as a lawsuit – in a Moslem court for the first time in history! – against police officers who conduct raids and excessive surveillance in bawdy-houses (the Durjoy Nari Shongho organization in Bangladesh)
- The creation of Daspu, short for "Das Putas" (whores), a fashion label aiming to provide recognition to the "prostitutes" of Rio de Janeiro (the Davida group in Brazil)
- The establishment of a mobile clinic and fruitful partnerships with hospitals and assistance programs for seropositive sex workers (Humanitarian Action in Russia)
- The development of self-defence and advocacy activities (the Odysseus organization in Slovakia)
- The organization of two national meetings, in 2002 and 2003, stimulating a desire among participants to form their own associations for defence of their rights (the Sex Worker Education and Advocacy Taskforce in South Africa)[9]
- Support and information offered to immigrants without papers or recently arrived in New York (the Urban Justice Center of the Sex Workers Project in the United States)

Even though abolitionists maintain that organizations defending the rights of sex workers represent only a not-credible minority, the awards, distinctions, and other gestures of recognition that these organizations have received prove otherwise.

How Much Longer Before We Acknowledge Sex Workers?
Not only is the concept of sex work an important theoretical advance, but it has made it possible to build a particular community, an environment

propitious to shaping the identity of the individuals concerned, articulating an ethics of openness, and laying the foundation for a social, critical, and political movement. "Probably the most important thing," wrote one of the organizers of Forum XXX, "is that all this work has helped us to create a community of sex workers – a community that's growing all the time" (Thiboutot 2006b, 24).

Thus, the community of sex workers is paving the way for a new mobilization in the field of sexuality. It is the idea of sexual community, at the core of this collective action, that makes sex workers credible, intelligible, and audible. By enacting a sense of belonging and a community-based point of view, anchored in motivations shared by a community with multiple experiences, the mobilization of sex workers sets critical discourses and practices in motion. And this community is making some waves within the most conservative fringe of today's society. Now, we must ask, how much longer before we acknowledge sex workers?

APPENDIX
Groups and Associations That Participated in Forum XXX

Africa
Danaya So – Association des femmes libres au Mali (Bamako, Mali)
Sex Worker Education and Advocacy Taskforce (Cape Town, South Africa)
Sisonke National Sex Workers Movement of South Africa (Cape Town, South Africa)

Americas
Asociación de Mujeres Meretrices de la Argentina (Buenos Aires, Argentina)
Bay Area Sex Work Advocacy Network (San Francisco, United States)
Different Avenues (Washington, United States)
HIPS – Helping Individual Prostitutes Survive (Washington, United States)
North American Task Force on Prostitution (New York, United States)
Prostitutes of New York (New York, United States)
Sex Workers Outreach Project – USA (San Francisco, United States)
SPREAD Magazine (New York, United States)
St. James Infirmary (San Francisco, United States)

Asia
Action for Reach Out (Hong Kong)
Collective of Sex Workers and Supporters (Taipei, Taiwan)
Durbar Mahila Samanwaya Committee (Culcutta, India)
Empower (Chiangmai, Thailand)
Gahum-Phils (Cebu City, Philippines)
Sex Workers Forum Kerala (Kerala, India)

Canada
519 Community Centre (Toronto)
2110 Centre for Gender Advocacy (Montreal)
Action Séro-Zéro (Montreal)
AIDS Calgary
Asian Community AIDS Services (Toronto)
Association des transexuel-les et travesti-es du Québec (Montreal)
Cactus Montréal
Canadian AIDS Society (Ottawa)
Canadian Guild for Erotic Labour (Toronto)
Canadian HIV/AIDS Legal Network (Toronto)
Catwoman – IRIS Estrie (Sherbrooke)

Centre d'amitié autochtone de Montréal
Coalition des organismes communautaires québécois de lutte contre le sida
Coalition pour les droits des travailleuses et travailleurs du sexe (Montreal)
Comité des personnes atteintes du VIH du Québec (Montreal)
Dopaine (Montreal)
Exotic Dancers Association of Canada
Kali Shiva AIDS Services (Winnipeg)
L'Anonyme (Montreal)
London Alliance to support Sex Trade Workers
Maggie's (Toronto)
Médecins du monde (Montreal)
Pair Aidants (Montreal)
Passages (Montreal)
Project 10 (Montreal)
Projet Vénus (Laval)
Prostitution Alternatives Counselling and Education (Vancouver)
Salam Queer Islamic Association (Canada)
Sex Professionals of Canada
Sex Workers Alliance of Toronto
Sex Workers Alliance of Vancouver
Stella (Montreal)
Stepping Stone (Halifax)
Two Spirit Circle of Edmonton Society

Europe
Aspasi (Geneva, Switzerland)
Cabiria (Lyon, France)
International Committee on the Rights of Sex Workers in Europe
   (Amsterdam, the Netherlands)
ROSEA – Riksorganisationen for Sex-och Erotikarbetare (National
   Organization for Sex and Erotic Workers) (Vantaa, Finland)

Oceania
New Zealand Prostitutes Collective (Wellington, New Zealand)
Scarlet Alliance (Sydney, Australia)
Sex Workers Outreach Project – Australia (New South Wales, Australia)
The Debbys Don't Do It for Free (Sydney, Australia)

International
International Union of Sex Workers
Network of Sex Work Projects

Notes

1 In Canada, two previous major conferences had involved sex workers. But both – *Challenging Our Images: The Politics of Pornography and Prostitution*, in Toronto in 1985, and *Quand le sexe travaille/When Sex Works*, in Montreal in 1996 – were criticized by some sex workers in attendance (Bell 1987; Sex Workers Alliance of Vancouver 1997, www.walnet.org/csis/groups/when_sex_works/index.html), who complained that their needs and concerns were not adequately reflected in the content and organization of these meetings. In contrast, all stages in the development and organization of Forum XXX focused on the interests of people who had experience with sex work. For example, these individuals were an active majority on the organizing committee, and 75 percent of registrations and activities were reserved for them. They represented diverse life contexts and working conditions. For more information, see Cantin et al. (2006).

2 Twenty-first-century neo-abolitionist feminists rush to discredit the approach taken by sex workers. For example, Yolande Geadah, author of *La prostitution un métier comme un autre?* (2003), posits that the discourses and arguments invoked by female sex workers' groups are neither legitimate nor true. In Geadah's view, they are "individual perspectives resulting from pecuniary interests and a partial and prejudiced vision of reality" (130, our translation). This charge against sex work has existed for a long time. For an analysis of its historical underpinnings, see Chapter 1.

3 Although stigmatization is a blatant phenomenon, little research has been devoted to its effects on the experience of female sex workers since the work done by Gail Pheterson in the 1970s (see Pheterson 1996). For more about concrete manifestations of stigma in Canada, see Bruckert (forthcoming); Canadian HIV/AIDS Legal Network (2005); Mensah and Lee (2006).

4 "Expressibility" is the desire of people to speak about their life and their work, to talk about themselves publicly or privately. The term covers various forms of discourse creation – such as disclosure, testimonial, and communication activities by organizations – that constitute a specific way of speaking about sexuality (Plummer 1995).

5 The anthropologist Paola Tabet (1987) has demonstrated the existence of a continuum in the forms of sexual relations between men and women involving an exchange. Tabet has found that promiscuity and retribution are not two fundamental and exclusive elements of "prostitution," but are observed also in marriage, for example. Her hypothesis is that compensation for sex acts introduces and maintains a sexual asymmetry that may subvert relations of patriarchal domination, and sex work would thus express a departure from the rules of ownership of women's bodies in different societies.

6 This expression for disclosure, short for "coming out of the closet," is used mainly by the gay, lesbian, bisexual, transsexual, and queer movements (Eribon 2003, 125).

7 Forum XXX was held at the Université du Québec à Montréal.

8 In that year, *Guide XXX* also won two Grafika awards for its excellence in graphic design in Quebec (the grand prize in the "Humanitarian Cause" category and the "Personal Favourite" award from juror Marc Serre).

9 The group later coordinated the organization of the first gathering of female sex workers in Africa, the African Sex Worker Conference, held in February 2009 in Johannesburg.

References

Bell, Laurie. 1987. *Good Girls/Bad Girls: Sex Trade Workers and Feminists*. Toronto: The Women's Press.

Bernier, Mélina. 2007. L'intervention sociale face aux travailleuses du sexe: résistance et mobilisation en regard des analyses dominantes de la prostitution au Québec. Master's thesis, Université du Québec à Montréal.

Bérubé-Gagné, Christiane. 1984. *Mémoire présenté à la Commission consultative sur le travail*. Montreal: Association féminine d'éducation et d'action sociale.

Bourdon, Marie-Claude. 2004. Quand les ménagères ménageaient. *Gazette des femmes* 25 (5), 30-32.

Bruckert, Chris. Forthcoming. Stigmatized Labour: Negotiating the Mark at Work. In *Stigma Revisited: Negotiations, Resistance and the Implications of the Mark Series*, ed. Stacey Hannem and Chris Bruckert. Ottawa: University of Ottawa Press.

Canadian HIV/AIDS Legal Network. 2005. *Sex, Work, Rights: Reforming Canadian Criminal Laws on Prostitution*. Toronto: Canadian HIV/AIDS Legal Network.

Canadian HIV/AIDS Legal Network and Human Rights Watch. 2006. Montréal Sex Workers and Jamaican LGBT Rights Activist Win 2006 Awards for Action on HIV/AIDS and Human Rights. Press release, 28 September, http://www.aidslaw. ca/publications/interfaces/downloadDocumentFile.php?ref=601.

Cantin, Émilie, Jenn Clamen, Jocelyne Lamoureux, Maria Nengeh Mensah, Pascale Robitaille, Claire Thiboutot, Louise Toupin, and Francine Tremblay, eds. 2006. *eXXXpressions: Forum XXX Proceedings*. Montreal: Stella.

Carrier, Micheline. 2005. 270 000 $ au groupe Stella pour une rencontre de 4 jours sur le "travail du sexe." sisyphe.org/article.php3?id_article=1777.

Crago, Anna-Louise. 2008. *Our Lives Matter: Sex Workers Unite for Health and Rights*. New York: Open Society Institute, Public Health Program: Sexual Health and Rights Project.

Debnath, Rama. 2006. A Kolkata Perspective. In *eXXXpressions: Forum XXX Proceedings*, ed. Émilie Cantin, Jenn Clamen, Jocelyne Lamoureux, Maria Nengeh Mensah, Pascale Robitaille, Claire Thiboutot, Louise Toupin, and Francine Tremblay, 28-30. Montreal: Stella.

Dorais, Michel. 2003. *Travailleurs du sexe*. Montreal: VLB.

Durbar Mahila Samanwaya Committee. 2000. *Manifeste des travailleuses du sexe de Calcutta*. Lyon: Le Dragon Lune, Cabiria Éditions.

Eribon, Didier, ed. 2003. *Dictionnaire des cultures gays et lesbiennes*. Paris: Larousse.

Foucault, Michel. 1976. *Histoire de la sexualité*, 1, *La volonté de savoir*. Paris: Gallimard.

Geadah, Yolande. 2003. *La prostitution un métier comme un autre?* Montreal: VLB Éditeur.

Gillies, Kara. 2006. Initiating with Our Peers Canada. In *eXXXpressions: Forum XXX Proceedings*, ed. Émilie Cantin, Jenn Clamen, Jocelyne Lamoureux, Maria Nengeh Mensah, Pascale Robitaille, Claire Thiboutot, Louise Toupin, and Francine Tremblay, 70-73. Montreal: Stella.

Goffman, Erving. 1963. *Stigma: Notes on the Management of Spoiled Identity*. New Jersey: Prentice Hall.

International Committee for Prostitutes' Rights. 1985. *World Charter for Prostitutes' Rights*. Amsterdam: ICPR, www.walnet.org/csis/groups/icpr_charter.html.

International Committee on the Rights of Sex Workers in Europe. 2005. *Manifeste des Sex Workers en Europe*. ICRSE, www.sexworkeurope.org/site/index.php?option =com_content&task=view&id=24&Itemid=201.

Kantorowicz, Liad. 2006. Solo Activism and Making Sex Work Visible. In *eXXXpressions: Forum XXX Proceedings*, ed. Émilie Cantin, Jenn Clamen, Jocelyne Lamoureux, Maria Nengeh Mensah, Pascale Robitaille, Claire Thiboutot, Louise Toupin, and Francine Tremblay, 46-48. Montreal: Stella.

Laliberté, Émilie, and Marie-Neige St-Jean. 2006. Transforming Individual Experiences into a Collective Stellar Project. In *eXXXpressions: Forum XXX Proceedings*, ed. Émilie Cantin, Jenn Clamen, Jocelyne Lamoureux, Maria Nengeh Mensah, Pascale Robitaille, Claire Thiboutot, Louise Toupin, and Francine Tremblay, 42-45. Montreal: Stella.

Mensah, Maria Nengeh, and C. Lee. 2006. *Tout ce que vous avez toujours voulu savoir sur le travail du sexe mais n'avez jamais osé demander. Cahier d'accompagnement à la formation*. Montreal: Stella and Services aux collectivités/UQAM.

Merriman, John M. 1994. *Aux marges de la ville: faubourgs et banlieues en France 1815-1870*. Paris: Seuil, "Univers historique" imprint.

Monnet, Corinne. 2006a. On Law and Order: Impacts of the French National Security Act – Sarkozy Law. In *eXXXpressions: Forum XXX Proceedings*, ed. Émilie Cantin, Jenn Clamen, Jocelyne Lamoureux, Maria Nengeh Mensah, Pascale Robitaille, Claire Thiboutot, Louise Toupin, and Francine Tremblay, 87-91. Montreal: Stella.

–. 2006b. A Lyon Perspective. In *eXXXpressions: Forum XXX Proceedings*, ed. Émilie Cantin, Jenn Clamen, Jocelyne Lamoureux, Maria Nengeh Mensah, Pascale Robitaille, Claire Thiboutot, Louise Toupin, and Francine Tremblay, 32-36. Montreal: Stella.

Mukerjee, Madhusree. 2006. The Prostitutes' Union: Among the Poor and Most Vulnerable, Smarajit Jana Has Found a Way to Slash the Incidence of HIV by Organizing Sex Workers as Any Other Labor Collective. *Scientific American*, www.sciam.com/article.cfm?id=the-prostitutes-union.

Namaste, Viviane K. 2000. *Invisible Lives: The Erasure of Transsexual and Transgendered People*. Chicago: University of Chicago Press.

–. 2005. *C'était du spectacle! L'histoire des artistes transsexuelles à Montréal, 1955-1985*. Montreal: McGill-Queen's University Press.

Paquet, Esther. 2007. *Pour des normes du travail à la hauteur*. Montreal: Au bas de l'échelle.

Parent, Colette. 2001. Les identités sexuelles et les travailleuses de l'industrie du sexe à l'aube du nouveau millénaire. *Sociologie et sociétés* 33 (1), 159-78.

Participants in Forum XXX. 2006a. Participants' eXXXpresssions on "Me and My Work": Pride, Coming Out and Personal Health and Safety. Summarized by Jenn Clamen. In *eXXXpressions: Forum XXX Proceedings*, ed. Émilie Cantin, Jenn Clamen, Jocelyne Lamoureux, Maria Nengeh Mensah, Pascale Robitaille, Claire Thiboutot, Louise Toupin, and Francine Tremblay, 53-55. Montreal: Stella.

–. 2006b. Participants' eXXXpressions on "Sex Work and Society": Diversity and Inclusion, Culture, Education, Mobilization and Organization. Summarized by Jenn Clamen. In *eXXXpressions: Forum XXX Proceedings*, ed. Émilie Cantin, Jenn Clamen, Jocelyne Lamoureux, Maria Nengeh Mensah, Pascale Robitaille, Claire Thiboutot, Louise Toupin, and Francine Tremblay, 75-89. Montreal: Stella.

–. 2006c. Participants' eXXXpressions on "Law, Policies and Human Rights." Summarized by Jenn Clamen. In *eXXXpressions: Forum XXX Proceedings*, ed. Émilie Cantin, Jenn Clamen, Jocelyne Lamoureux, Maria Nengeh Mensah, Pascale Robitaille, Claire Thiboutot, Louise Toupin, and Francine Tremblay, 101-2. Montreal: Stella.

Pheterson, Gail. 1996. *The Prostitution Prism*. Amsterdam: Amsterdam University Press.

Ping Pong. 2006. How Personal Experiences in Thailand and Burma Facilitated the Creation of Empower Projects. In *eXXXpressions: Forum XXX Proceedings*, ed. Émilie Cantin, Jenn Clamen, Jocelyne Lamoureux, Maria Nengeh Mensah, Pascale Robitaille, Claire Thiboutot, Louise Toupin, and Francine Tremblay, 51. Montreal: Stella.

Plummer, Kenneth. 1995. *Telling Sexual Stories: Power, Change and Social Worlds*. London: Routledge.

Poulin, Richard. 2008. Prostitution. In *Questions de sexualité au Québec*, ed. Joseph Josy Lévy and André Dupras, 400-21. Montreal: Liber, "Auteurs UQAM" imprint.

Puckmai, Pornpit. 2005. *Human Rights Award – We Congratulate One of Our Peers*, http://www.scarletalliance.org.au/issues/human-rights/.

Reynaga, Éléna Eva. 2006. The Drive for a Union: Why We Needed It and Why It Works. In *eXXXpressions: Forum XXX Proceedings*, ed. Émilie Cantin, Jenn Clamen, Jocelyne Lamoureux, Maria Nengeh Mensah, Pascale Robitaille, Claire Thiboutot, Louise Toupin, and Francine Tremblay, 66-68. Montreal: Stella.

Sprinkle, Annie. 2008. Stopping the Terror: A Day to End Violence against Prostitutes. *On the Issues: The Progressive Woman's Magazine* 18, www.ontheissues magazine.com/cafe2.php?id=21.

Tabet, Paola. 1987. Du don au tarif: les relations sexuelles impliquant une compensation. *Les Temps Modernes* 42 (490), 1-53.

Thiboutot, Claire. 2006a. Designing Our Future. In *eXXXpressions: Forum XXX Proceedings*, ed. Émilie Cantin, Jenn Clamen, Jocelyne Lamoureux, Maria Nengeh Mensah, Pascale Robitaille, Claire Thiboutot, Louise Toupin, and Francine Tremblay, 126-30. Montreal: Stella.

–. 2006b. A Montreal Perspective. In *eXXXpressions: Forum XXX Proceedings*, ed. Émilie Cantin, Jenn Clamen, Jocelyne Lamoureux, Maria Nengeh Mensah, Pascale Robitaille, Claire Thiboutot, Louise Toupin, and Francine Tremblay, 23-27. Montreal: Stella.

Toupin, Louise. 2005. Voir les nouvelles figures du féminisme et entendre leurs voix. In *Dialogues sur la troisième vague féministe*, ed. Maria Nengeh Mensah, 74-87. Montreal: Remue-ménage.

Weeks, Jeffrey. 2000. The Idea of Sexual Community. In *Making Sexual History*, 182-93. Cambridge: Polity Press.

Young, Iris Marion. 1990. The Ideal of Community and the Politics of Difference. In *Feminism/postmodernism*, ed. Linda Nicholson, 300-23. New York: Routledge, "Thinking Gender" imprint.

Clandestine Migrations by Women and the Risk of Trafficking   **5**

LOUISE TOUPIN

When asked what image spontaneously comes to mind when they think of the expression "trafficking or smuggling women," many people would answer, "third world prostitutes" or slaves of Mafia traffickers. Others might think of the "white slave trade." Such top-of-mind responses, reflecting the most common portrayals of the phenomenon, have circulated for more than a hundred years.

A horrifying picture is brought to mind, in which women and innocent children are abused by Mafia networks and transported and sold into sexual slavery in the most squalid brothels. To a degree, the current discourse is an extension of the one on "white slave trade" at the turn of the last century and stems from a similar panic around women's sexuality. The only thing that has changed is "the direction of the circulation" of individuals (Guillemaut 2008, 152, our translation). A century ago, "white slave trade" referred to "white women" being exported from Europe, whereas today "trafficking in women" concerns women from the South or the East entering the West.

Many of the sensationalist images conveyed in the media and promoted by a good number of proponents of a prohibitionist or abolitionist[1] approach to "prostitution" (an approach that extends from the Christian right to certain fringes of the women's movement and the border police) are based on studies with disputable methodologies, inaccurate generalizations of figures extrapolated from extreme cases reported in the newspapers, or imprecise samples.[2] The type of information – necessarily biased – that emerges is based also on a bleak picture of women. Along with children, women are seen as eternal victims to be saved from the clutches of their predators – in this case, "foreign" traffickers – rehabilitated, and helped to return "home," the idea being that there's no place like home (Agustín 2003), especially when one is a "poverty-stricken foreigner."

Yet, more and more female migrants and groups defending their rights are demanding that this colonialist and infantilizing image of women be done away with. They emphasize that although some may be victims of trafficking during their travels, they are also, as migrants, subjects and agents of their own lives and migrations. Many of them reject being reduced simply to the identity of victim, which has the perverse effect of making all migrant women immediately suspect of being "prostitutes," homogenizing their plural migratory experiences, and threatening their right to migrate and to travel freely around the world. Nor do many see themselves in the dominant discourse about them or in the image that the media reflect of them. A growing number of empirical studies conducted among women who have migrated from the South to the North come to this conclusion.

In this chapter, I give an overview of the perspectives of some of these empirical studies (see Agustín 2008, 49, note 60; see also Bilger, Hofman, and Jandi 2006; Blanchet 2002; Cabiria 2004; Crago 2008; Doezema 2000; Dottridge 2007; Empower 2005; Guillemaut 2002, 2004, 2006, 2008; Kempadoo 2005; Kempadoo and Doezema 1998; Oso Casas 2003; Sanghera 2005; Yuet-Lin and Koo 2005). In doing so, I want to highlight the heuristic wealth of approaches that, in illustrating the complexity of the phenomenon of human trafficking from the viewpoint of migrants' experiences, show that these migrants' discourse on their journey has little in common with the dominant discourse on trafficking: "The words of these migrants tell us not that there are no abuses or problems [in migratory experiences] but that 'trafficking' is a woefully inadequate way to conceptualise them" (Agustín 2008, 48).

After a brief historical overview of the "genealogy" of the current representation of "trafficking in" and "smuggling of" women and of the issues defining these phenomena, I make use of some field studies conducted with migrants in order to answer six questions: (1) How do women find themselves in a situation of being trafficked? (2) Who are the "traffickers?" (3) What is the global scope of trafficking? (4) Does trafficking of women exist in Canada? (5) How effective are international anti-trafficking mechanisms, and have they reduced the number of victims? (6) What do female sex workers' groups advocate in this regard?

First, I look at the "genealogy" of current representations of "trafficking in" or "smuggling of" women. These representations have always been sensationalized in the media, and the issue at stake has always been women's sexuality.

"Trafficking in Women": Genealogy of a Term

At the turn of the twentieth century in Europe, the tabloid press was feathering its nest with reports of supposed abductions and sales of underage European girls, who were said to be transported outside their home countries for the purpose of "sexual servitude." The expression "white slave trade" was thus invented, by analogy – falsely, in the opinion of many today (Chaumont and Wibrin 2007) – with the African slave trade.

Associated in reality with the vast wave of emigration that swept millions of Europeans to the four corners of Earth in the early twentieth century (Corbin 1990), this "white slave trade," according to a current historiographic revision, was in large part a myth and a phenomenon of moral panic, playing out against a background of eugenics and a "crusade for purity" (see Chaumont 2009; Corbin 1990; Doezema 2000; Walkowitz 1980). The problem of the "white slave trade" is today considered "more significant by the fear-ridden literature that conveyed it than by the reality that it concealed. It was the crossroads of all the obsessions of the period, a subject on which the most balanced minds of the era lost their bearings" (Corbin 1990, 275). As the twentieth century progressed, however, the definition of the "white slave trade," associated at first with "international trafficking in *minor* girls," began to be broadened to include foreign "prostitution" involving *adult* women, even consenting ones.

This extrapolation of the notion of "trafficking in women" is also found in the 1949 United Nations' *Convention for the Suppression of the Traffic in Persons and of the Exploitation of the Prostitution of Others*, which replaced and recast the preceding international accords signed in the wake of the "white slave trade" phenomenon.[3] In this convention, trafficking in women was defined as and identified with "prostitution." Any notion of coercion or consent was absent from this definition. The first article clearly conveyed the convention's intention, which was to "punish any person who, to gratify the passions of another: (1) procures, entices or leads away, for purposes of prostitution, another person, even with the consent of that person; (2) exploits the prostitution of another person even with the consent of that person." The keeping of a brothel was also to be penalized. The convention criminalized "third parties" in order to block movements of women for "prostitution" within or beyond the borders of a country. As they were deprived of all autonomy to make decisions, women undertaking this activity, associated with minors and children, were considered victims to be protected, including from themselves.

In fact, however, the national laws that were promulgated to extend international agreements regarding trafficking in women had the effect of giving states more power to repress female sex workers than to penalize "traffickers." Among other perverse effects of these laws was that of preventing women from migrating alone.[4]

The 1949 convention thus represented the typical abolitionist approach to "prostitution." The original expression, "white slave trade," now transformed into "trafficking in women," became the international aspect of the more general "evil" that is "prostitution."[5]

In reality, this was just one aspect of a much broader issue: the migration of women. Some women might have been trafficked for purposes other than sex, including for domestic or agricultural work, for work in the textile or garment industry or in the restaurant or food-production business, as exotic dancers, and for arranged marriages. The reduction of the trafficking in women to "prostitution" concealed what was happening in other sectors of the black-market economy, in which women, and men, and children might be trafficked.

The current conflation of trafficking in women with "international prostitution" is to a large extent equivalent to the same moral panic that was seen at the beginning of the last century (Chaumont 2009; Doezema 2000). Today, as in the past, it is again the sexuality of migrant women that is seen as frightening. As they did with regard to white slavery, "the most balanced minds of the era [have] lost their bearings" and the question of trafficking in women is similarly instrumentalized.

Trafficking Equals "Prostitution": A Contested Conflation

After 1949, public attention to trafficking in women abated. It returned to the headlines in the 1980s, with the development of sex tourism and feminist debates on pornography, especially in the United States. The 1949 convention, with its definition of trafficking in women and countermeasures, up to then not truly contested, was brought into question.

In the 1980s, some feminist circles wanted to consolidate and reinforce the 1949 convention by giving it real teeth (for example, by criminalizing not only "third parties" but also customers). On the other hand, the convention was attacked by others, particularly the associations of female sex workers that had begun to form in the 1970s, for its perverse effects, which included "punishing rather than protecting women," "denying women the status of adult and the right to migrate," and denying female sex workers the right to economic and sexual self-determination (Pheterson 1989, 13-14). Such effects could only accentuate these women's marginalization and stigmatization. Furthermore, a number of components of the process that could lead to trafficking were excluded from the definitions in the 1949 convention, which focused exclusively on "prostitution."

A document put out by the International Organization for Migration (1995) noted that human trafficking "covers a wide variety of situations, not all of which involve illegal migration or exploitation ... For example, a person who pays thousands of dollars to be transported illegally to a Western country may face little exploitation or see it as the price s/he is willing to pay to secure his or her long-term future." Furthermore, a person trafficked within a country may not have entered that country illegally. The IOM also deplored the confusion that existed in the 1949 convention between "prostitution" in general and trafficking: not all foreign "prostitutes" are trafficked, and the trade in female migrants does not always involve "prostitution." The UN Special Rapporteur on violence against women noted, "While all trafficking is, or should be, illegal, all illegal migration is not trafficking" (Coomaraswamy 1997, par. 12).

The 1980s: Feminists Mobilize

The publication in 1979 of *Female Sexual Slavery*, by the American sociologist Kathleen Barry, was an explosive catalyst for feminist activism on trafficking in women.[6] At the instigation of Barry, along with Charlotte Bunch and Shirley Castley, the International Feminist Network Against Sexual Slavery and Trafficking in Women, with an abolitionist perspective reflecting the theoretical basis of Barry's book, was founded in Rotterdam in 1983. The network's goal was described by Bunch (1984, 71, our translation): "The network's first actions will be directed against prostitution, trafficking in women, sex tourism, and their connections with violent acts such as rape, sexual mutilation, incest, physical abuse, forced marriage, dowries and purchasing of brides, pornography, and the torture of female political prisoners."[7]

In Gail Pheterson's (1989, 18) view, "The event inspired a snowballing of alliances between women inside and outside of the sex industry," which led to the formation, in 1985, of the International Committee for Prostitutes' Rights, of which Pheterson was co-founder and co-director. In that year and the following year, world congresses of female sex workers were held in the Netherlands and Belgium, respectively, following which a World Charter for Prostitutes' Rights was written. The charter demanded, in contrast to the abolitionist approach, that "all aspects of adult prostitution resulting from individual decision" be decriminalized.[8]

Similar initiatives undertaken at the same time in Southeast Asia contributed to the formation, in 1994, in Chiangmai, Thailand, of the Global Alliance Against Traffic in Women (GAATW), supported by a large number of female sex workers and women's rights groups. This coalition's philosophy of intervention is based on the principle of migrant women's right to self-determination (which induces a differentiation between "prostitution" as work and forced "prostitution").[9] Trafficking in women is therefore identified with violation of women's rights in the course of their travels and migrations, and it is seen as synonymous with coercive recruitment conditions, the transportation of women, and women's labour (when they arrive at the destination), in all informal economic sectors.

This perspective on trafficking is broader than the abolitionist one of identifying trafficking in women with "prostitution." GAATW advocates for a broader definition of trafficking and presents it as a cycle or process, and for inclusion of a human rights framework within the international regulations; this framework will apply standards to the treatment of victims of trafficking and serve as a guide for various states in this regard (see Global Alliance Against Traffic in Women 1999).

In the meantime, the neo-abolitionist network created by Kathleen Barry in 1983 became, in 1991, the Coalition Against Trafficking in Women (CATW), standard-bearer for worldwide neo-abolitionist feminism.[10] In its lobbying, CATW demanded that the sanctions set out in the 1949 convention be strengthened and victims be protected, and it opposed any distinction between trafficking and "prostitution" in a new definition of trafficking. Rather, CATW wanted the new definition to specify that all "prostitution," in itself, was a violation of human rights and that because of this it had to be "abolished."

During the 1990s, CATW and GAATW, each in its own way, applied pressure to have the definition of trafficking altered to fit their view of its meaning. Their intention was to influence the drafters of the Convention against Transnational Organized Crime, known as the Palermo Convention, signed in December 2000, and its two protocols regarding the smuggling of and trafficking in persons (see United Nations 2000).[11] The convention provided an opportunity for a new definition of these activities to be enshrined in international law. Here are some aspects of this definition.

Smuggling and Trafficking: Two Different Realities

In common parlance, until recently the terms "smuggling" and "trafficking" were used interchangeably. Since the signature of the Palermo Convention, however, a distinction has been established between them in two of the convention's "additional protocols":

1   Smuggling in persons concerns the clandestine (and therefore illegal) transportation of migrants (willingly) from one country to another, in return for material or financial compensation. This is illegal crossing of borders.

2   Trafficking in persons[12] is defined by three key elements:

   a) The relocation of a person (activities linked to recruitment, relocation, or crossing borders)

   b) Constraint or deception (threats, use of force, fraud, abuse of authority or of a situation of vulnerability)

   c) Exploitation of labour (the intention to exploit, once the person arrives at the destination: forced labour, slavery and similar practices, debt bondage, sexual exploitation)

The distinction between smuggling of and trafficking in persons is important because it is now recognized that one may legally enter a country and, upon arrival, be subjected to trafficking. Conversely, one may enter a country illicitly yet voluntarily and not be subjected to trafficking. The illegal crossing of borders (smuggling of migrants) is one thing; trafficking is another.[13]

The absence of consent given with full knowledge of what is at stake is another aspect of the definition of trafficking (see note 12). The Palermo Convention does not specify the terms of "sexual exploitation" or "exploitation of prostitution of the other," which leaves free rein to the legislatures of the signatory countries[14] and, as a consequence, to controversy over the definition.

How Do Women Find Themselves in a Situation of Being Trafficked?

Men, women, transgenders, and transsexuals migrate for all sorts of reasons, including economic ones. Migration models are multiple and differentiated by sex (Morokvasic 1986, 73), notably due to the persistence of the sexual division of labour (Kofman 2003, 90). Thus, people migrate for various reasons: they may face violence or discrimination at home, they may wish to escape a subservient position, they may experience displacement following war or a natural disaster, or they may have political cause. For many years, family reunification has not been the only model for female migration.

More and more women, all over the world, find themselves alone at the head of a family (Bissilliat 1996) – immediate or extended – and must migrate to support this family because the labour market in their own country offers few or no plausible opportunities. It is now estimated that half of all migrants worldwide are female, and that a growing proportion are migrating independently (Dahinden et al. 2007; United Nations 2005, 9).

In destination countries (those in Europe, as well as the United States), these new worldwide migratory movements have generally resulted in increased vigilance at or closing of borders, even though these same countries are the biggest users of foreign labour, notably women who provide carework and personal (domestic and sexual) services, sectors that are generally not well regulated, or not even completely legal. And on the margins of this picture are available migrants, although they cannot always migrate legally. This situation leads to conditions propitious to the development of fraudulent recruitment, abuse, and exploitation. To this amalgam of factors exposing women to the risk of trafficking must be added the sexism inherent in national laws.

Women who have few rights in their own country run a greater risk of finding themselves in difficult predicaments when they migrate. For instance, for many female migrants around the world, obtaining papers that legalize their position "may depend on their status as a wife or daughter, and a change in the family may lead to a loss of access to healthcare or force them into an illegal situation" (Verschuur 2004, 15, our translation). The sexism of certain national laws may force women to use clandestine intermediaries in order to migrate. The absence of a right to full and complete citizenship is therefore one of the major determinants of the risk of being trafficked. In fact, the United Nations rapporteur on trafficking in women and on women's migration observes that absence of rights and lack of freedom are the main causes of trafficking in women (Coomaraswamy 1997, par. 54).

This makes it relevant, when studying the question of migration, to adopt a framework of analysis that takes into account the interlaced power relations that structure the lives of migrants (sexism, heterosexism, racism, xenophobia, neocolonialism, class and sex relations, stigmatization, and so on). Trafficking in and smuggling of women must therefore be repositioned in a South-North (or East-West) labour framework in a migratory situation and in a framework of sexed migration. Discrimination against women is at the core of the migratory process, notable in the limited range of jobs to which they have access, in both countries of origin and destination countries. These jobs parallel traditional female employment ghettoes in the private sphere, in unregulated sectors – caregiving and domestic and sexual services – that do not provide protection or social rights.

Discrimination against women would also be inscribed within the very organization of trafficking and smuggling, which is itself a "sexed" operation.[15] This has led Jacqueline Oxman-Martinez and Jill Hanley (2007, 6) to state that "trafficking is a human rights issue, as well as a gender issue." One must take care, in adopting such a perspective, not to homogenize migrant women within the indistinct category of potential "victims" by linking them with children, as each woman has a unique path and develops her own survival and resistance strategies.

Who Are the "Traffickers"?

A common representation of the "trafficker" is that of "foreigner," linked to one or more international organized crime networks, who subjects his prey – mostly women and children – to slavery for the purpose of "prostitution." The label "trafficker" is another good case of homogenizing vocabulary. A number of field studies (Agustín 2008; Guillemaut 2004; Oso Casas 2003; Sanghera 2005) demonstrate that under this label are found a multitude of individuals, some of them ready to use illegal means to facilitate the migration of people who cannot migrate legally. A variety of actors and intermediaries organize undocumented migration.

Given the gradual closing of the borders of Northern countries to Southern immigrants, people who nevertheless wish to migrate must do business with, and make payments to, intermediaries to obtain the information, services, and documents (fares, work permits, and so on) essential to their plans. Some people must indebt themselves to do so. Often, members of the migrant's family or her friends or loved ones supply part or all of the money needed for the various phases leading to crossing a border, which establishes close links between future migrants and these "facilitators" (who are women in many cases). Marriage may even be part of the migration mechanism.

Then, other intermediaries and providers of smuggling services arrange for transportation and arrival at the destination; once migrants have arrived, they will need to deal with still other intermediaries during their stay. These different phases of the journey are not *necessarily* taken care of by organized crime, as is popularly believed. At least, this is the observation of researchers who conducted in-depth interviews with clandestine migrants in Austria:[16]

> Our research indicates that the market for human smuggling services is in most cases not dominated by overarching mafia-like criminal structures that have monopolised all smuggling activities from the source to the destination country. Rather, in many regions there exists a complex market for highly differentiated smuggling services offered by a multitude of providers from which potential migrants can choose. (Bilger, Hofmann, and Jandi 2006, 64)

There is thus a "chain of informal networks assisting migrations" (Agustín 2008, 29) active on the migration black market. Such a context inevitably creates conditions propitious to exploitation and abuse of all sorts, including the risk of being trafficked. However, given the chain of intermediaries necessary for clandestine migration, speaking of "traffickers" as a homogeneous group would be an improper generalization today. The presumed network of Mafia traffickers is, in reality, most often "the guy next door" (Sanghera 2005, 15). Studies show that, in many countries, it is this type of informal mechanism that is usually targeted in anti-trafficking measures, while the true exploiters and abusers of female migrants go unpunished (Crago 2003, 26; Dottridge 2007, 11).

Like the media discourse on smuggling and trafficking, the overgeneralization of the word "trafficker" is apparently part of the moral panic that surrounds, as it always has, the sexuality of migrant women (Agustín 2008, 41). Obviously this does not mean that criminal organizations are not involved in the illegal migration sector; their influence, however, is vastly overestimated, according to the serious data available on this clandestine activity.

What Is the Global Scope of Trafficking?

Since trafficking is an illegal activity, the data that are purported to assess its scope are extremely approximate and subject to manipulation by the various parties with a vested interest in the issue. For example, the number of illegal female entries into countries is often combined with the number of women who are victims of trafficking, resulting in an over-estimation of the phenomenon that feeds indirectly into "an anti-migratory and sexist discourse" (Cabiria 2004, 23, our translation).

Estimates of the overall number of women and girls who are "victims of sexual trafficking," can be similarly skewed and range from four million (Coalition des luttes contre l'exploitation sexuelle 2005; Legardinier 2002, 12) to "some hundred thousand" (Panos Institute 1998, cited in Dupont 2005, 150). Here, "some hundred thousand women and girls sold and bought" is conflated with "four million people who are subjected to undefined trafficking" (Dupont 2005, 150, our translation). In reality, "the data available [with regard to trafficking for the purpose of prostitution] emanate from international agencies relayed by the press, but no methodology as to their formulation is revealed," notes Françoise Guillemaut (2008, 158, our translation), an anthropologist who has done fieldwork on the subject in Europe.

To illustrate the difficulty with quantifying the phenomenon, Guillemaut reports on the case of the number of women who were supposedly going to be "trafficked" for the purpose of "prostitution" during the Football World Cup in Berlin in June 2006. CATW advanced the figure of 40,000 and managed to obtain 140,000 signatures for an international protest. Yet "[n]o report by police, or by an NGO in the field, or by experts mandated by the International Organization for Migration was able to supply evidence of the truth of the facts after the demonstration. According to these sources,[17] five cases (four women and one man) out of the 40,000 feared victims of trafficking were identified by the German federal police over the period" (Guillemaut 2008, 159, our translation).[18] Even before they began, the 2010 Winter Olympics in Vancouver were subjected to similarly inflated figures. The disinformation methods used remain to be scrutinized and analyzed.[19]

Such exaggerations of the scope of sex trafficking are now beginning to be deconstructed. The British daily *The Guardian* (20 October 2009) investigated the discourse on the question of sex trafficking in the United Kingdom and concluded that it is "dominated by ideology" and a "model of disinformation." Dissecting the anatomy of this "wave of disinformation," the newspaper observes, "It flows through exactly the same channels as the now notorious torrent about Saddam Hussein's weapons."[20]

In the view of Kamala Kempadoo (1998, 15), the absence of reliable data on generally clandestine and illegal activities makes it almost impossible to come to any well-supported conclusion regarding the scope of the phenomenon. Any conscientious researcher must deal cautiously with the enormous gaps in the data and manipulate prudently the statistical apparatus used; all figures are only estimates.

The same observations hold for the extent of involvement of organized crime in the smuggling of women, which is largely exaggerated by the press. Chris Bruckert and Colette Parent have reviewed the documentation on the links between human trafficking and organized crime. They, too, were stymied by the absence of reliable data on trafficking. They found only "highly divergent and unreliable estimates of the dimensions of human trafficking and of the involvement of organized crime in these activities." Moreover, they observed that there "was no coherent theoretical framework that structures reflections and empirical research on the issue" (Bruckert and Parent 2002, 15, 7, our translation).

Is There Trafficking in Women in Canada?

The trafficking phenomenon remains extremely difficult to evaluate, including in Canada. As long as methodologies for studies on the subject remain secret, the numerical data drawn from them will always be highly questionable. For example, according to figures recently compiled by the Royal Canadian Mounted Police (RCMP) (cited in Oxman-Martinez and Hanley 2007, 7), every year more than 600 people are victims of trafficking in Canada "in the context of sexual exploitation," and a higher number, "more than 800," are trafficked "into markets such as domestic work, factory work, and agricultural work." Also, "between 1,500 and 2,200 people are trafficked from Canada into the United States" (unpublished RCMP document, quoted in Oxman-Martinez and Hanley 2007, 7). This RCMP study remains unpublished to this day; there is no way to judge the reliability or validity of the data presented in it. We therefore cannot draw precise conclusions from it.

Furthermore, the study by Oxman-Martinez and Hanley (2007, 11-13) on human trafficking describes the situation of migrants who have entered Canada legally but may eventually be terribly exploited. Canadian government programs that issue temporary work permits apparently offer "fertile ground for exploitation, and many people may end up working under slavery conditions"(Oxman-Martinez and Hanley 2007, 11). For example, the Seasonal Agricultural Workers Program and the Live-In Caregiver Program put people in the position of being temporary workers, obligatorily linked to employers; this makes them very vulnerable, as they can denounce their working conditions only at risk of being deported.

In a teaching guide that it prepared, the Association des aides familiales du Québec states, "Flaws in the LCP (Live-in Caregiver Program) pave the way for trafficking, smuggling, and modern slavery upstream and downstream of the recruitment process" (Osmani 2008, 27, our translation). The association also deplores the "tendency to prioritize and differentiate crimes associated with trafficking, smuggling, and modern slavery: rapes and sexual abuse may appear morally more horrible and unbearable than exploitation of caregivers" (Osmani 2008, 45, our translation).

How Effective Are International Anti-trafficking Mechanisms? Have They Reduced the Number of Victims?

The Palermo Convention and its two protocols on trafficking and smuggling address these two questions as problems of international organized crime and illegal migration. They put human trafficking and smuggling on the same footing as drug and arms trafficking. Human trafficking and smuggling may occur in a number of industries, and the sex industry is only one among them.

From a crime-control perspective, then, the intention of the convention and the protocols is to strengthen the laws to make it easier for governments to share information on organized crime and, as a result, to identify and prosecute traffickers. The objection to such a crime-control perspective by defenders of human rights and women's rights around the world, however, is that they do not address the root causes of illegal migration for the purposes of work and thus render ineffective the anti-trafficking measures devised and push these migration activities further underground.[21]

These groups also condemn the Palermo Convention for not being an effective instrument for the defence of human rights and deplore in particular the weak protection that it provides for witnesses. In fact, the only individuals covered by the provisions in the convention and the two protocols that offer protection and assistance to victims of trafficking are those who agree to cooperate with the police and testify against the traffickers. Those who refuse to do so receive no protection at all; most of them will be deported (as will, in fact, a good number of those who agree to cooperate).

The Palermo Convention is criticized for not including a human rights framework for victims of trafficking, such as those proposed by GAATW, one of the coalitions involved in formulating the *Human Rights Standards for the Treatment of Trafficked Persons* (see Global Alliance Against Traffic in Women et al. 1999). A GAATW report (Dottridge 2007) studied the impact on human rights of measures set out in the protocol on trafficking in eight countries.[22] Its conclusion was clear: "The anti-trafficking framework has done little good for the trafficked person and great harm to migrants and women in the sex industry" (Dottridge 2007, 20). One of the report's main criticisms is that states devote more effort to identifying and apprehending people suspected of trafficking than to eliminating the forms of exploitation recognized in the protocol (Dottridge 2007, 12).

Thus, a number of countries criminalize the intermediaries who help to move people, rather than penalizing the exploiters of migrants. Furthermore, the people most affected by these measures are women and children, in part because the very title of the protocol[23] singles out these two groups. In some countries, the prevention of trafficking is the reason given to justify measures taken to impede migration. Other countries do not identify men as victims of trafficking; men are therefore ineligible to receive services otherwise available to female victims of trafficking.

All of the measures clearly affect migrant women, including female sex workers, disproportionately to migrant men. Although the new definition of "trafficking" was adopted internationally in 2000, some countries continue to use/apply the old definition – the one in the 1949 convention – which identifies trafficking with "prostitution." This means that victims of other forms of trafficking or exploitation are left without protection or assistance. Anti-trafficking measures thus serve very often to justify a series of instruments designed to suppress sex work in general, rather than to attack specific situations of "forced prostitution" and other forms of exploitation mentioned in the Palermo Protocol (Dottridge 2007, 17).

The United States is typical in this regard. In 2001, the US launched a global anti-trafficking crusade that had an impact on a number of countries around the world. In 2003, the Bush administration decided to stop financing HIV/AIDS-prevention programs if the beneficiary organizations did not explicitly condemn "prostitution." As a result of this decision, government funding agencies such as the United States Agency for International Development (USAID) are no longer providing funding to organizations started up by female sex workers. These organizations had to take a sort of pledge in order to receive money.[24]

In 2004, the Canadian government was asked to do something similar. Some "thirty personalities" from Quebec, many of them eminent feminists from the scholarly and art sectors, instigated a campaign to have the government "require" groups defending female sex workers to which it granted funding make "a formal commitment to fight prostitution" (Audet and Carrier 2004, A9, our translation). It is difficult not to see the influence of the Bush administration's crusade on this "appeal to the government of Canada."

The Bush policy was based on the premise that decriminalization of sex work would encourage trafficking in women, even though this premise was challenged by another American governmental agency, the Government Accountability Office; the premise apparently was not based on any precise data (US Government Accountability Office 2006, 25).[25] The strategy adopted by the Bush administration to fight trafficking was found to be counter to human rights. Allowing people at risk of being trafficked to exert these rights necessitates, apparently, a completely different approach.[26]

Conclusion: What Do Groups Defending Migrant Female Sex Workers Advocate?

A number of groups defending female sex workers have pointed to the following problem: up to now, the mechanisms set up to combat human trafficking have targeted mainly "prostitution"; by ignoring the existence of other forms of trafficking, they reduce human trafficking to sex work in general. What is more, in targeting "prostitution," they are incapable of distinguishing between sex trafficking, on the one hand, and sex work in a migratory situation, on the other hand, thus confusing sex trafficking and sex work, whatever the conditions of practice (Yuet-Lin and Koo 2005, 151). As a consequence, the problems of migrant female sex workers are conflated with those of victims of sex trafficking. Many organizations that use this approach are incapable of responding adequately to the real needs of female migrants of any kind.

As Empower (a group defending female sex workers in Thailand) has observed, since 2000, the international community's interest in the issue of trafficking in women has led to the creation of a number of non-governmental organizations that want to take advantage of the financing that has become available for provision of support services to victims, despite the fact that many of these NGOs have little experience in the areas of migration, labour, sex work, or women's rights. The inexperience of these organizations and their lack of contact with the community of female sex workers are detrimental to female migrants. For example, the organizations are unable – deliberately or not – to differentiate between trafficked women and migrant women or to determine categories of different needs for women and children. The conflation of women's needs and children's needs is so common that women are frequently treated as if they were children (Empower 2005, 154).

This demonstrates the need for another approach, focused on the work of women in a migratory situation, such as the approach adopted by groups defending the rights of female migrants, including migrant female sex workers. As Empower notes, "Anti-trafficking dialogue and groups have yet to consider us as anti-trafficking workers and human rights defenders even though the numbers of women and children we assist far outweigh the handful of women and children serviced by the recognized anti-trafficking groups. Instead, we are ourselves caught up in the 'rescues and repatriation' [missions]" (quoted in Stella 2006).

In effect, female sex workers' groups have become leaders in the fight against forced labour, debt bondage, and minors working in the sex industry. For example, the twenty-seven female sex workers' self-regulation committees in Sonagachi, a red-light district in Kolkota, have helped "hundreds of women and underaged girls forced into sex work against their will to escape" (Stella 2006). The Sonagachi project is an initiative founded in 1992 by a cooperative of female sex workers who are activists in HIV prevention and the defence of female sex workers' rights. This project, "unanimously hailed internationally" (Piot and Cravero 2006, 206, our translation), has been deemed by the United Nations Development Program to be exemplary in its field.[27]

"People don't want to be rescued, they want to be safe. They don't want to go back, they want to go on" (quoted in Kempadoo 2005, xvi): This is the heartfelt cry of many of the female workers and migrants "stuck in these 'rescue and repatriation' missions," who find themselves detained in forced-rehabilitation centres, where their rights and free-doms are flouted.[28] This is why groups defending female sex workers advocate a completely different approach, based on their empowerment (Agustín 2003) and their participation in all steps of the search for and adoption of solutions concerning them.

As trafficking is considered a violation of women's rights in the course of their migrations, the services that assist them must aim not to repatri-ate them at all costs (unless this is what they want), but to support them in their migratory process and help them recover their independence – for example, by obtaining stay documents and work permits for them and denouncing violence against them, whether it is by police, inter-mediaries in their migration, or employers. The services offered to female trafficking victims should have the goal of enabling them to exercise their legal and social rights, supporting their right to work – whether or not the society considers this work legitimate – and offering the protection that international labour laws grant to all workers.

Such an approach – a human rights approach – has been championed for more than twenty years by GAATW, among other organizations. As Jyoti Sanghera (2007, x), one of GAATW's directors, notes, this new perspective has changed the "anti-trafficking paradigm" that had prevailed previously; more particularly, it separates trafficking and "prostitution" and makes coercion one of the characteristics of trafficking; it distinguishes trafficking from illegal migration; by broadening the definition of trafficking, it portrays it as a process and a cycle whose purposes may be, aside from sexual exploitation, exploited and forced work, slavery-like practices, and forced marriage. The definition of trafficking adopted by the Palermo Protocol, which is based on the complexity of the phenomenon, owes much to the efforts that GAATW has made on the international level, Sanghera emphasizes. A good number of groups representing female sex workers all over the world support GAATW's perspective.[29]

Notes

1 These two labels refer to a single legal parameter: criminalization. For the different legal regimes regarding "prostitution," see Chapter 2. For different approaches to "prostitution," see Chapter 1.

2 For some critiques of the methodological bias in such studies, see Chaumont and Wibrin (2007); Clausen (2007); Crago (2003); Deschamps and Souyris (2008); Mathieu (2007, 2009); Mensah (2003); Toupin (2006).

3 The preceding international accords were:

- the *International Agreement for the Suppression of the White Slave Traffic*, ratified by twelve countries in 1904, in which governments agreed to prevent "the procuring of women or girls for immoral purposes abroad";
- the *International Convention for the Suppression of the "White Slave Traffic*," ratified in 1910 by thirteen countries, which broadened the scope of the 1904 agreement to include trafficking in women within national borders;
- the *International Convention for the Suppression of the Traffic in Women and Children*, signed in 1921; and
- the *International Convention for the Suppression of the Traffic in Women of the Full Age*, aimed at punishing people who organized the traffic in adult women, whether they were consenting or not, signed in 1933.

4 See Doezema (2000). She cites the example of Greece, which, in 1912, barred women younger than twenty-one from travelling abroad without a special permit.

5 The preamble of the 1949 convention is clear: "Prostitution and the accompanying evil of the traffic in person for the purposes of prostitution are incompatible with the dignity and worth of the human person and endanger the welfare of the individual, the family, and the community." See http://www2.ohchr.org/english/law/trafficpersons.htm.

6 The following outline of the formation of international feminist coalitions against trafficking in women is drawn from Toupin (2002, 15-23).

7 For the network's history and theoretical strategic bases, see Barry, Bunch, and Castley (1984).

8 For the history of this mobilization of "prostitutes" and the two world congresses, see Pheterson (1989). The World Charter for Prostitutes' Rights can be accessed at http://www.walnet.org/csis/groups/icpr_charter.html.

9 For an overview of the alliance's activities and orientations, see www.gaatw.org.

10 For an overview of the network's activities, see its Web site, www.catwinternational.org.

11 The protocols concerned are the *Protocol against the Smuggling of Migrants by Land, Sea and Air, Supplementing the United Nations Convention against Transnational Organized Crime* and the *Protocol to Prevent, Suppress and Punish Trafficking in Persons, Especially Women and Children, Supplementing the United Nations Convention against Transnational Organized Crime*.

12 Article 3a of the *Protocol to Prevent, Suppress and Punish Trafficking in Persons* states, "'Trafficking in persons' shall mean the recruitment, transportation, transfer, harbouring or receipt of persons, by means of the threat or use of force or other forms of coercion, of abduction, of fraud, of deception, of the abuse of power or of a position of vulnerability or of the giving or receiving of payments or benefits to achieve the consent of a person having control over another person, for the purpose of exploitation. Exploitation shall include, at a minimum, the exploitation of the prostitution of others or other forms of sexual exploitation, forced labour or services, slavery or practices similar to slavery, servitude or the removal of organs." Article 3b states, "The consent of a victim of trafficking in persons to the intended exploitation set forth in subparagraph (*a*) of this article shall be irrelevant where any of the means set forth in subparagraph (*a*) have been used."

13 However, some researchers feel that it can sometimes be very difficult, given the plurality of actors and intermediaries needed to organize a migration, to make a clear distinction between legal and illegal migration activities and to "clearly distinguish legal migration from trafficking" (Bruckert and Parent 2002, 10, our translation).

14 The "interpretative notes" state, "The protocol addresses the exploitation of the prostitution of others and other forms of sexual exploitation only in the context

of trafficking in persons. The terms 'exploitation of the prostitution of others' or 'other forms of sexual exploitation' are not defined in the protocol, which is therefore without prejudice to how States parties address prostitution in their respective domestic laws" (United Nations 2008, 347).

15 Françoise Guillemaut (2007, 100, our translation) observes, "The way in which 'trafficking' is organized corresponds schematically to the sexual division of regular work found in legal sectors of the economy: to men go the information circuits, means of transportation, tools (for the fabrication of false documents), weapons (violence), and capital. To women goes labour with no rights."

16 For other research on this subject in other European countries, see Neske and Doomernik (2006).

17 Guillemaut (2008, 159) cites *Experience Report on Human Trafficking for the Purpose of Sexual Exploitation and Forced Prostitution in Connection with the 2006 Football World Cup in Germany* (5006/0/07 REVI, Council of the European Union, 19 January 2007) and *Trafficking in Human Beings and the 2006 World Cup in Germany* (International Organization for Migration, September 2006).

18 See also Libertad, Une légende urbaine: les 40 000 "prostituées" d'Europe de l'Est importées en Allemagne pour la coupe du monde de football (published by Nicole Nepton, 24 July 2006), cybersolidaires.typepad.com/ameriques/2006/07/une_lgende_urba.html.

19 Consider the fear campaign endorsed by the Salvation Army: "The Truth Isn't Sexy," www.thetruthisntsexy.ca. See also Global Alliance Against Traffic in Women (2011).

20 "In the story of UK sex trafficking, the conclusions of academics who study the sex trade have been subjected to the same treatment as the restrained reports of intelligence analysts who studied Iraqi weapons – stripped of caution, stretched to their most alarming possible meaning and tossed into the public domain. There, they have been picked up by the media who have stretched them even further in stories which have then been treated as reliable sources by politicians, who in turn provided quotes for more misleading stories." Nick Davies, Prostitution and Trafficking – The Anatomy of a Moral Panic, *The Guardian*, 20 October 2009, www.guardian.co.uk/uk/2009/oct/20/trafficking-numbers-women-exaggerated. See also, in the same issue, the other section of the inquiry: Nick Davies, "Inquiry Fails To Find Single Trafficker Who Forced Anybody into Prostitution," www.guardian.co.uk/uk/2009/oct/20/government-trafficking-enquiry-fails/print.

21 On this subject, see the various contributions in Kempadoo (2005).

22 The countries studied were Australia, Bosnia-Herzegovina, Brazil, India, Nigeria, Thailand, the United Kingdom, and the United States.

23 *Protocol to Prevent, Suppress and Punish Trafficking in Persons, Especially Women and Children, supplementing the United Nations Convention against Transnational Organized Crime.*

24 See "Taking the Pledge," a thirteen-minute video produced by the Network of Sex Work Projects on the harm that this policy did to female sex workers all over the world: www.nswp.org. See also Sarah Boseley and Suzanne Goldenberg, Le Brésil rejette les conditions étatsuniennes pour l'aide contre le sida, *The Guardian*, 4 May 2005, trans. Édith Rubinstein, cybersolidaires.typepad.com/ameriques/2005/05/le_brsil_rejett.html.

25 "For example, the 2005 Trafficking in Persons Report asserts that legalized or tolerated prostitution nearly always increases the number of women and children trafficked into commercial sex slavery, but does not cite any supporting evidence" (US GAO 2006, 25, quoted in Dottridge 2007, 18).

26 For a critique of anti-trafficking campaigns that have impacts on anti-immigration practices, see, among others, Sharma (2003).

27 See Self-Regulatory Boards: Kolkota's Sex Workers Show the Way, in *Responses to Trafficking and HIV/AIDS in South Asia* (United Nations Development Program 2003): "Sex workers in Domjur say that the existence of the Self-Regulatory Board in the red-light area and the links between Board members and the Panchayat (local government council) have not only curbed trafficking but also brought them other benefits – like piped water and sanitation facilities" (quoted in Crago 2008, 37). For more information on the project and the group administering it in India (DMSC), see cybersolidaires.typepad.com/direct/2005/05/travail_du_sexe.html. For other initiatives of this type that have received public recognition, see Chapter 4.

28 For an operation of this type in Cambodia in 2008, see the video *Caught between the Tiger and the Crocodile*, sexworkerspresent.blip.tv/#1165299.

29 GAATW's Web site gives an excellent overview of its anti-trafficking activity. See www.gaatw.org.

References

Agustín, Laura Maria. 2003. Forget Victimisation: Granting Agency to Migrants. *Development* 46 (3): 30-36.

–. 2008. *Sex at the Margins: Migration, Labour, Markets and the Rescue Industry.* London and New York: Zed Books.

Audet, Élaine, and Micheline Carrier. 2004. Appel au gouvernement du Canada: Une trentaine de personnalités demandent la décriminalisation des personnes prostituées, mais non la prostitution. *Le Devoir,* 3 December, A9. http://www.sisyphe.org/article.php3?id_article=1368.

Barry, Kathleen. (1979) 1984. *Female Sexual Slavery.* New York and London: New York University Press.

Barry, Kathleen, Charlotte Bunch, and Shirley Castley, eds. 1984. Féminisme international: Réseau contre l'esclavage sexuel. Rapport de l'atelier féministe international contre la traite des femmes. Rotterdam, 6-15 April 1983. *Nouvelles questions féministes* 8.

Bilger, Véronike, Martin Hofmann, and Michael Jandi. 2006. Human Smuggling as a Transnational Service Industry: Evidence from Austria. *International Migration* 44 (4): 59-93.

Bissiliat, Jeannine, ed. 1996. *Femmes du Sud, chefs de famille.* Paris: Karthala.

Blanchet, Thérèse. 2002. *Beyond Boundaries: A Critical Look at Women Labour Migration and the Trafficking Within.* Dhaka: Drishiti Research Center. Submitted to USAID. www.walnet.org/csis/papers/BEYOND.DOC.

Bruckert, Chris, and Colette Parent. 2002. *La "traite" des êtres humains et le crime organisé: examen de la littérature.* Ottawa: Gendarmerie royale du Canada, Direction des services de police communautaires contractuels et autochtones, recherche et évaluation.

Bunch, Charlotte. 1984. Stratégies et organisation du Réseau contre l'esclavage sexuel. *Nouvelles questions féministes* 8: 11-18.

Cabiria. 2004. *Femmes et migrations en Europe. Stratégies et empowerment.* Lyon: Le Dragon Lune Éditions.

Chaumont, Jean-Michel. 2009. *Le mythe de la traite des blanches.* Paris: La Découverte.

Chaumont, Jean-Michel, and Anne-Laure Wibrin. 2007. Traite des Noirs, traite des Blanches: même combat? *Cahiers de recherches sociologique* 43: 121-32.

Clausen, Vincent. 2007. *An Assessment of Gunilla Ekberg's Account of the Swedish Prostitution Policy,* www.sexworkeurope.org/de/resources-mainmenu-189/category/16-sweden.

Coalition des luttes contre l'exploitation sexuelle. 2005. *Déclaration de la CLES,* www.lacles.org/index.php?option=com_content&view=article&id=3:declaration&catid=3 :qui-nous-sommes&Itemid=6.

Coomaraswamy, Radhika. 1997. *Integration of the Human Rights of Women and the Gender Perspective. Violence Against Women, Report of the Special Rapporteur on Violence Against Women, Its Causes and Consequences on Trafficking in Women, Women's Migration and Violence Against Women, Submitted in Accordance with Commission on Human Rights Resolution 1997/44.* United Nations, Economic and Social Council, 29 February.

Corbin, Alain. 1990. *Women for Hire: Prostitution and Sexuality in France after 1850,* trans. Alan Sheridan. Cambridge: Harvard University Press. Originally published in 1982 as *Les filles de noces. Misère sexuelle et prostitution au xixe siècle.* Paris: Flammarion, Collection "Champs."

Crago, Anna-Louise. 2003. Les dessous de la lutte contre la traite des femmes et des enfants. *ConStellation* 8 (1): 22-30.

–. 2008. *Our Lives Matter: Sex Workers Unite for Health and Rights.* New York: Open Society Institute, Public Health Program: Sexual Health and Rights Project.

Dahinden, Janine, Magdalena Rosende, Natalie Benelli, Magaly Hanselmann, and Karine Lempen. 2007. Migrations: Genre et frontières – frontières de genre. *Nouvelles questions féministes* 26 (1): 4-13.

Deschamps, Catherine, and Anne Souyris. 2008. *Femmes publiques. Les féminismes à l'épreuve de la prostitution*. Paris: Éditions Amsterdam.

Doezema, Jo. 2000. Loose Women or Lost Women? The Reemergence of the Myth of "White Slavery" in Contemporary Discourses of "Trafficking in Women." *Gender Issues* 18 (1): 23-50.

Dottridge, Mike. 2007. *Collateral Damage: The Impact of Anti-Trafficking Measures on Human Rights around the World*. GAATW, www.gaatw.org.

Dupont, Sylvie. 2005. Les millions et moi. *La vie en rose. Hors série*, 150-52. Montreal: Remue-ménage.

Empower. 2005. A Report by Empower Chiangmai on the Human Rights Violations Women Are Subjected to When "Rescued" by Anti-trafficking Groups. In *Trafficking and Prostitution Reconsidered: New Perspectives on Migration, Sex Work, and Human Rights*, ed. Kamala Kempadoo, 153-54. Boulder: Paradigm Publishers.

Global Alliance Against Traffic in Women. 2011. *What's the Cost of a Rumour? A Guide to Sorting Out the Myths and the Facts about Sporting Events and Trafficking*, http://www.gaatw.org/publications/WhatstheCostofaRumour.11.15.2011.pdf.

Global Alliance Against Traffic in Women, Foundation Against Trafficking in Women, and International Human Rights Law Group. 1999. *Human Rights Standards for the Treatment of Trafficked Persons*, http://gaatw.org/books-pdf/hrs-engl1.pdf.

Guillemaut, Françoise. 2004. Trafics et migrations de femmes, une hypocrisie au service des pays riches. *Hommes et migrations* 1248: 75-87.

–. 2006. Victimes de trafic ou actrices d'un processus migratoire? Saisir la voix des femmes migrantes prostituées par la recherche-action (enquête). *Terrains et travaux* 1 (10): 157-76.

–. 2007. Femmes migrantes non européennes et secteur du service: Travail du sexe/travail domestique, une alternative sans choix? Presentation at the colloquium *Nouvelles dynamiques migratoires: Activités régulières et irrégulières sur le marché du travail européen*, workshop Industrie du sexe et trafics: Une voie pour les migrantes? Nice, 6-8 December, http://calenda.revues.org/nouvelle9378.html.

–. 2008. Mobilité internationale des femmes, échanges économico-sexuels et politiques migratoires: La question du "trafic." In *Femmes, genre, migrations et mondialisation: Un état des problématiques*, ed. Jules Falquet, Aude Rabaud, Jane Freedman, and Francesca Scrinzi, 147-68. Paris: Université Paris Diderot, Paris-7, CEDREF, Colloques et travaux series.

Guillemaut, Françoise, ed. 2002. *Femmes et migrations. Les femmes venant d'Europe de l'Est*. Lyon: Cabiria, Le Dragon Lune.

International Organization for Migration. 1995. *Trafficking and Prostitution: The Growing Exploitation of Migrant Women from Central and Eastern Europe*. Migration Information Program, www.iom.int.

Kempadoo, Kamala. 1998. Globalizing Sex Workers' Rights. In *Global Sex Workers: Rights, Resistance and Redefinition,* ed. Kamala Kempadoo and Jo Doezema, 1-28. New York: Routledge.

Kempadoo, Kamala, ed. 2005. *Trafficking and Prostitution Reconsidered: New Perspectives on Migration, Sex Work, and Human Rights.* New York: Paradigm Publishers.

Kempadoo, Kamala, and Jo Doezema, eds. 1998. *Global Sex Workers: Rights, Resistance and Redefinition.* New York: Routledge.

Kofman, Eleonore. 2003. Genre et migration internationale: Critique du réductionnisme théorique. In *Genre, travail et migrations en Europe,* ed. Madeleine Hersent and Claude Zaidman, 81-97. Paris: Université de Paris Diderot, Paris 7, CEDREF, Colloques et travaux series.

Legardinier, Claudine. 2002. *Les trafics du sexe: Femmes et enfants marchandises.* Paris: Les Essentiels Milan.

Mathieu, Lilian. 2007. *La condition prostituée.* Paris: Éditions Textuel.

–. 2009. Ce que le mélange entre expertise et militantisme peut produire de pire ... *Contretemps,* contretemps.eu/socio-flashs/ce-que-melange-entre-expertise -militantisme-peut-produire-pire.

Mensah, Maria Nengeh. 2003. Visibilité et droit de parole des travailleuses du sexe: Abolition ou trafic d'un espace citoyen? *Canadian Woman Studies/Les Cahiers de la femme* 22 (3-4): 66-71.

Morokvasic, Mirjana. 1986. Émigration des femmes: Suivre, fuir ou lutter. *Nouvelles questions féministes* 13: 65-73.

Neske, Matthias, and Jeroen Doomernik. 2006. Cluster Introduction. Comparing Notes: Perspectives on Human Smuggling in Austria, Germany, Italy, and The Netherlands. *International Migration* 44 (4): 39-58.

Osmani, Farida. 2008. *Trafic, traite et esclavage moderne des aides familiales migrantes au Québec.* Teaching guide. Montreal: Association des aides familiales du Québec.

Oso Casas, Laura. 2003. Migration et trafic des femmes latino-américaines en Espagne: Service domestique et prostitution. In *Genre, travail et migrations en Europe,* ed. Madeleine Hersent and Claude Zaidman, 163-87. Paris: Université de Paris Diderot, Paris 7, CEDREF, Colloques et travaux series.

Oxman-Martinez, Jacqueline, and Jill Hanley. 2007. *Human Trafficking = Trata de personas = La traite des personnes.* Montreal: CRI-VIFF.

Pheterson, Gail. 1989. *A Vindication of the Rights of Whores.* Seattle: Seal Press.

Piot, Peter, and Kathleen Cravero. 2006. Les femmes et le sida. In *Le livre noir de la condition des femmes,* ed. Christine Ockrent, 197-232. Paris: XO Éditions.

Sanghera, Jyoti. 2005. Unpacking the Trafficking Discourse. In *Trafficking and Prostitution Reconsidered: New Perspectives on Migration, Sex Work, and Human Rights,* ed. Kamala Kempadoo, 3-24. Boulder: Paradigm Publishers.

–. 2007. Preface: Lessons from the Poetry of Departures. In *Collateral Damage: The Impact of Anti-Trafficking Measures on Human Rights around the World,* ed. Mike Dottridge, vii-x. GAATW, www.gaatw.org.

Sharma, Nandita. 2003. Travel Agency: A Critique of Anti-trafficking Campaigns. *Refuge: Canada's National Newsletter on Refugees* 21 (3): 53-65.

Stella. 2006. *Sex Workers and Trafficking.* Montreal: Stella. http://chezstella.org/docs/ConsSIDAtraffic.pdf.

Toupin, Louise. 2002. *La question du "trafic des femmes." Points de repère dans la documentation des coalitions féministes internationales anti-trafic.* Working document. Montreal: Stella/IREF-Relais-femmes.

–. 2006. Analyser autrement la "prostitution" et le "trafic des femmes." *Recherches féministes* 19 (1): 153-76.

United Nations. 2000. *United Nations Convention against Transational Organized Crime and the Protocols Thereto.* www.unodc.org/unodc/en/treaties/CTOC/index.html#Fulltext.

–. 2005. *2004 World Survey on the Role of Women in Development. Women and International Migration.* New York: United Nations, Department of Economic and Social Affairs, Division for the Advancement of Women.

United Nations, Office on Drugs and Crime. 2008. *Travaux Préparatoires of the Negotiations for the Elaboration of the United Nations Convention against Transnational Organized Crime and the Protocols Thereto.* http://www.unodc.org/pdf/ctoccop_2006/04-60074_ebook-e.pdf.

US Government Accountability Office. 2006. *Human Trafficking: Better Data, Strategy, and Reporting Needed to Enhance U.S. Anti-trafficking Efforts Abroad.* Report No. GAO-06-825 to the Chairman, Committee on the Judiciary and the Chairman. Committee on International Relations, House of Representatives, Washington, www.gao.gov/news.items/d06825.pdf.

Verschuur, Christine. 2004. Un regard genré sur les migrations. In *Femmes en mouvement. Genre, migrations et nouvelle division internationale du travail,* ed. Fenneke Reysoo and Christine Verschuur. Geneva: Institut universitaire d'études et de développement. UNESCO, graduateinstitute.ch/webdav/site/genre/shared/Genre_docs/2865_Actes2004/01-c.verschuur.pdf.

Walkowitz, Judith R. 1980. *Prostitution in Victorian Society: Women, Class and the State.* New York: Cambridge University Press.

Yuet-Lin, Yim, and Anita Koo. 2005. Redefining Trafficking in NGO Practices. In *Trafficking and Prostitution Reconsidered: New Perspectives on Migration, Sex Work, and Human Rights,* ed. Kamala Kempadoo, 149-52. Boulder: Paradigm Publishers.

Biographies

Chris Bruckert (PhD in sociology) is an associate professor in the Department of Sociology at the University of Ottawa. She has contributed to numerous research projects exploring different sectors of the sex industry. Her ethnographic research with female nude dancers has captured the complexity of the concept of women's work when it is transposed into the world of the professional stripper. She has herself been a sex worker and, from this point of view, she brings to light the fact that these workers are the authors, and not the objects, of their experiences. In this book, she describes the skills necessary to be a sex worker and the challenge that female sex workers face on a daily basis, including the heritage of prohibitionists and moralizers.

Patrice Corriveau (PhD in sociology) is an associate professor in the Department of Criminology at the University of Ottawa; previously, he was a senior analyst of criminal policy at the Department of Justice Canada. His research areas have included a sociological history of suicide in Quebec, issues involved in the repression of homosexuality and homophobia, street gangs (including the theme of "juvenile prostitution"), the criminalization of people with HIV/AIDS, and child pornography on the Internet. He has acquired a keen comprehension of laws on procuring. In this book, he presents various legal models for control of "prostitution" and their limitations. Advocating the decriminalization of sex work, he deconstructs the false arguments advanced by proponents of a repressive approach.

Maria Nengeh Mensah (PhD in communications) is a full professor at the School of Social Work and the Feminist Research Institute of the Université du Québec à Montréal. An expert in the issue of HIV/AIDS among women and the means to counter the effects of their marginalization, she has conducted extensive research among people who work in the sex industry. Her research interests include the articulation between popular and ideological discourses, as well as the use of public testimonials for addressing social problems that combine health, sexuality, and marginality. Engaged in community environments, she works closely with groups of sex workers in Canada and in other countries. For example, she has participated in the application of community solutions to dismantle the dynamics of social exclusion faced by sex workers: the training of social workers on the issue, the production of health-protection and -promotion tools, and the organization of an international forum of sex workers and their allies, Forum XXX. Her overview of sex workers' activism and initiatives in this book is based on this forum, held in Montreal in 2005.

Colette Parent (PhD in criminology) is a full professor in the Department of Criminology at the University of Ottawa. Her research area encompasses women and criminality – specifically, the development of feminisms in criminology, violence against female spouses, and penal interventions among women and sex work. For the past twenty years, she has conducted empirical research on sex work based in the street, massage parlours, erotic establishments, and dance bars, and on the work of male, female, and transsexual escorts. Her objective is to contribute to the development of sociological parameters associated with sex work as it is experienced as a trade in the services sector. Writing in 1994, she emphasized the need to think of the question of "prostitution" from within the world of female sex workers. In this book, she perceptively describes the current debate over sex work as well as the social stigma attached to, and the impact of current law on, this type of work.

Louise Toupin (PhD in political science) is an independent researcher and lecturer on feminist studies in the Department of Political Science at the Université du Québec à Montréal and the Institute of Women's Studies at the University of Ottawa. Her early teaching, research, and publications focused on the history and evolution of the feminist movement, its theories and currents, and an epistemological critique of certain frames of analysis. She then became interested in new figures in the women's movement, including female sex workers. She has written on the issues and challenges that the questions of "prostitution" /sex work and "trafficking in women" pose to the theorization and practice of feminism. Her analyses in this book highlight the critical reversals in this field of research, including those that reformulate, from the point of view of those living it, the problem of "prostitution" and human trafficking in light of the right to mobility and the right to work.

Index

Printed and bound in Canada

Set in Myriad and Sabon by Artegraphica Design Co. Ltd.

Copy editor and proofreader: Jillian Shoichet

Indexer: Christine Jacobs